The Best Kept Secret of The New Rich!

"The Fortune Hunter System!"

by
Steven A. Houseman

All rights reserved under International and Pan-American Copyright Conventions. Published in the United States by New Start Publications, Inc., Sterling, Virginia
Copyright ©1987 by Steven A. Houseman

Library of Congress Cataloging in Publication Data
Steven A. Houseman

TITLE: The Best Kept Secret of The New Rich!
    I. Title.

ISBN 0-915451-07-7

Manufactured in the United States of America
9 8 7 6 5 4 3 2 1

All rights reserved. This book or any part thereof may not be reproduced in whole or in part without permission in writing from publisher.

TABLE OF CONTENTS
"The Fortune Hunter System!"

Chapter		Page
Intro	The Best Kept Secret of The New Rich!......	1
1	Don't Envy These Millionaires, Join Them. I'll Show You How........................	9
2	I Made $400,000.00 The First Time Out. But You Can Do Better........................	21
3	Free Advertising.........................	27
4	How To Make Free Advertising Work For You	31
5	P.I. Advertising Can Make You A Fortune. But Sometimes You're Better Off Using Your In-House Agency........................	37
6	Discounts Means Money In Your Pocket. Use Your In-House Agency....................	45
7	How To Purchase Discounted Air Time.....	51
8	Hot Tips For Big Bucks....................	59
9	How To Make A TV Commercial..........	63
10	How To Make A Sound Track In A Recording Studio........................	69
11	How To Make The Visual Half of Your Commercial.............................	81
12	How To Make A Product Commercial......	87
13	Three Tips For TV Station Filming.........	95
14	Untapped Hong Kong Manufactures........	99
15	Untapped American Importers.............	103
16	The S.R.D.S. Spot Television Directory.....	149

We're Celebrating -On TV!

Introduction

The Best Kept Secret of The New Rich!

You know your Million is "out there" waiting for you. But you're having trouble finding it. Does that sound familiar? Well, you're right about one thing: there is a million dollars (and more!) that could be your's, but you've probably overlooked where it might be. Before I explain that it's under your nose, let me tell you how it got there. I'll also tell you how you can learn to get your million. Then you, too, can get in on the New Wealth that's being created.

Everyone knows that the pace of life is quickening. The power behind the acceleration is communication. TV, as familiar as it is - yes, that TV right in your living room - is the rapid communicator. In the financial sense, it's changing American life more then ever before.

A sociologist in the 1960's once said, "the medium is the message" and at the time not many people knew what he meant. Well, as far as TV is concerned, the medium has met its message - and the word is MONEY!

So what has this to do with your million? Let me fill you in on recent developments and current situations. There are Active Forces acting on New Elements which are producing New Wealth. This is what the picture looks like:

3 Active Forces
  -the search for wealth
  -knowledge about wealth
  -Money

3 New Elements
  -the national atmosphere of the Get Rich momentum
  -the financial entrepreneur/personality with money secrets
  -television broadcasters and cable channels with air-time to sell

In the world of wealth, three Active Forces are at work. The first force is the average American in search of riches, a new life, a better tomorrow. This Active Force is a constant one. The second force, knowledge, belongs to those who have it, knowledge that is put to work for self-benefit. The third force, Money, has properties that we're all familiar with. Money: it attracts us, pulls us - and, also, it sometimes seems to escape us, it moves away.

These three Active Forces are always at work. They have always been there. They share a dynamic relationship. But something has been changing how they interact lately. The three New Elements, in just the last two years, have radically re-shaped the three Active Forces.

Nationwide, more than a dozen self-made millionaires have heeded the call to spread their secrets of wealth via television - and, most particularly, through cable channels. Technology of the 80's, satellite communications, has created a national momentum: the New Wealth.

The first new element, the Get Rich momentum, is moving like a fast train. The movement for self betterment has always been a force at work, but never on the scale - and at the speed - it operates at now. The second element is the self-made millionaire. Oh, the millionaire has existed before, but not like today's new breed.

Today's self-made millionaire, with his secrets of New Wealth, doesn't come from the old-wealth elite or the expensive business schools. These people are renegades in a sense. They are not stuffy bankers, oil barons, or blue chip bluebloods. The millionaires of New Wealth are so-called "average" people - they just happen to have added millions of dollars to their bank accounts. They are excited, and exciting, individuals. They are proud and happy about their wealth. They have discovered unique, simple, tested methods for making money. They have no stuffy, incomprehensible explanations of how they make their money. It's not in them to hide their joy or energy. Sharing their experiences with wealth is a common, natural characteristic.

The final, third New Element has really put it all together to re-shape Wealth. Television, every man's medium, has

IT'S SHOWTIME

become the teacher of a generation. Television is the learner's tool. It helps us reach for the riches we seek.

You can judge for yourself. Deregulated television rules and the birth of cable has been a surprising field. Going up against the established networks hasn't been easy. Cable channels and independent broadcasters have innovatively programmed to survive. The New Wealth broadcasters, renegades themselves, have befriended the average American with popular, well-produced shows, many of them spreading the knowledge gratefully to the cable viewer.

"We ought to build a monument to the person who got the idea to put self-improvement programming on television," says one TV executive. Certainly everyone has tremendously gained from the so-called Get Rich shows. A single half hour of programming can cost anywhere from $2,000 to $3,000. There are specialists who sell TV time. Station owners made $200 million last year selling their stations' time. One station, Group W Satellite Communications, has six New Wealth programs. Group W themselves made $5 million last year from such broadcasting.

The New Wealth system has been born. Numerous persons have found new ways to find riches and the word is spreading. Recent developments in the economy and in technologies are making millionaires out of "ordinary" people. The changing pace of finance is like an express train to new frontiers of wealth.

And what is this New Wealth that's being created? Who are the New Millionaires? You've probably seen or heard about one aspect of this already. Have you ever caught a TV show about millionaires and their secrets? Did you ever ask yourself, "What do these New Millionaires know about money that I don't?" So, you watch, and here's what's happening:

You're sitting there at home watching TV. It may be late on a weeknight or during the day on the weekend. Flipping the channels, you come across a show, major network or cable, and some guy is telling you that you can get rich. So, you watch awhile. The guy may be talking real estate, products, or services, but the message is clear: he has a way of using both existing systems and new techniques that have made him a millionaire. And he's there to tell others how they, too, can benefit from his experience and knowledge.

Any amount of time spent watching can benefit the viewer. And, for those who are really serious about making big money, people determined to change their lives forever, additional courses or seminars can be had for the price of a paycheck. A home-study course, priced from $99 to $350, costs a minute fraction of the return. It's like spending one penny to make a hundred dollars.

When these shows aren't being broadcast, the author-lecturers tour the U.S. with one and two-day seminars. All of the home-study courses explained on the half hour to two hour programs can be ordered by calling a toll-free number. Even credit cards can be used for the ordering and money-back guarantees are always the rule. That's how intent the broadcasters are about getting the word out.

Listen, don't be a dollar short because you're a day late. Learn what's there, NOW, and never be caught a dollar short - or even a million dollars - ever again.

A lot of Big Money is Old Money, but thousands of people have become millionaires only recently with New Money. This new class of millionaires has come along in just the last two years, given birth by the explosion of Get-Rich-Quick advisors seen on broadcast stations and cable channels around the country.

New programming on the airwaves is changing the way people think of money. Countless Americans have become financially independent following the simple methods dispensed from shows like "A Millionaire's Secrets to Wealth" and "The Millionaire Maker." More than three million viewers tune in weekly to the U.S.A., Lifetime, Financial News Network, and S.P.N. networks for useful, legal, money-making advice. The techniques are explained not in old boy financial-ease, but in easy to follow, easy to understand language. (32 Million Housholds Have Cable TV, out of the 82 million people who own televisions.)

The factual success and documented millions of the new teachers can be experienced on more than two dozen shows which appear regularly each week. These are not show business personalities. They are ordinary people, though ad-

mittedly millionaires, who have discovered basic knowledge. They use existing systems in a creative manner. They combine the desire and determination to succeed. They apply themselves to consistent, simple plans. The millionaire's abundant pleasure and energy in life is obvious. That's what independent wealth can do for a man.

Of course, there is skepticism or criticism from the establishment. Such reactions stem from injured pride and territorial protection instincts: 1) they didn't know making money could work so easily and simply themselves, and 2) they want it all for themselves, the elite, and they are offended that just anyone can do it. Through television programming and home-study courses, not years of college and generations of wealth. Home viewers can receive tips and money-making knowledge on a wide variety of topics: no-money down real estate, tax-sale properties, rental property income, and government loans. People without previous business experience can learn to understand and use bank credit, credit card cash, cash-flow, or how to obtain riches through distressed properties, auctions, and low interest agency-guaranteed loans.

The established old-boy system of wealth in this country loves to make you quake at the prospect of car payments, making the rent, or buying your child a new pair of shoes. Most workers trade their weekly labor for a couple of hundred dollars and worry about meeting bills which tie them up financially for the rest of their lives. The "price of living" is big compared to the small return of wages. And that's the way the old-boy wealthy would like to keep it.

But the teachers and preachers of New Wealth aren't talking about investments, franchises, or risking your livlihood for up-in-the-air changes in your life. Everything they have to share with you is knowledge that anyone can use "in your spare time" and without leaving your present job or hometown.

Who are these people and what secrets do they have? You'll meet them in these exclusive personal profiles of riches and success. Their secrets? There are no secrets at all because these people are boldly passing the word along. They're teaching others their big-money techniques, sharing the information withheld from you by the established traditional fortune-makers. And, frankly, most of the old-boy rich don't even know most of the things these people can teach.

Obviously, the medium has met its message. The economical method of rapidly spreading new money-making techniques by way of television has developed just in time to meet the fast-paced nature of high finance. And television has long been the average citizen's most familiar learning and entertainment center. Yet, whereas a generation ago millions of people were raised on television, now a new generation, one of newly made millionaires, are raising themsleves up thanks to the messages of more than a dozen New Wealth teachers.

Chapter One
Don't Envy These Millionaires, Join Them. I'll Show You How!

Profile: Tony Hoffman, 44; California

Tony Hoffman might well be called the Ambassadore to the many TV teacher-millionaire Kings. Hoffman practices his brand of shuttle-diplomacy from the comfort of a television studio. He's a millionaire in his own right, but you get more for your money with Tony and his show, "Everybody's Money Matters." Hoffman and his guests are seen daily on two cable channels: on the Satelite Program Network (SPN) from 11 p.m. to 1 a.m. and the Lifetime cable channel from 1 a.m. to 3 a.m. (on weeknights in both cases).

Someone once called Tony Hoffman "the Phil Donahue of Finance" and the title couldn't be better applied. In a single two-hour telecast, Tony brings numerous millionaires together for interviews and discussions of money-making techniques. Hoffman gives the viewer the chance to do the choosing between his guests' varying advice, seminar offers, and home-study courses. Each guest can attest to being a self-made millionaire, demonstrating to anyone who tunes in that the United States is now, more than ever before, the land of opportunity.

So-called "secrets" - maneuvers used by those in the know, bankers, investors, Wall Street barons - are unveiled nightly. Tony Hoffman is perhaps single-handedly spreading the secrets of wealth faster than a score of his guests. Tony's own company, National Superstar, plans a franchised chain of education centers in shopping malls around the country. These centers will allow memberships with unlimited access to enriching, money-making programs and self-improvement videotapes.

Tony's course in life has long pointed the way towards financial independence and spreading the word to many others with the same drive and ambition. More than 15 years ago, Hoffman read William Nickerson's "How I Turned $1,000 into $3 Million in Real Estate in My Spare Time" while recuperating in a hospital from a back operation. This was while he was still back in his hometown, Brooklyn, New York. Before he was out of the hospital, Tony pooled $20,000 from three doctors and the hospital chef into a partnership to buy an apartment complex.

Not then, and not since, did he use his own money. Within six years, 22 more deals were put together. By then, Tony had moved to sunny Phoenix, Arizona, and continued numerous other no-money down deals, buying and selling real estate.

After Tony spent four years on the lecture circuit with Albert Lowry (author of "How You Can Become Financially Independent by Investing in Real Estate"), Tony established one of the first traveling seminars (National Superstar). Now, National Superstar is his own independent company. 1985 was the year he began his career on TV with Everybody's Money Matters."

Hoffman's estimated net worth now exceeds $10 million. He now lives in California, with his wife and two children. He even owns a nearby 240 acre plantation raising jojoba (a very in-demand native crop) which could earn Tony $1,000 to $2,000 per acre. But that's just his "money on the side." Tony's show, "Everybody's Money Matters," is still his bread and butter.

Tony embodies the millionaire, wearing dollar-sign shaped, diamond-studded rings, one on each hand. This young at heart wizard is tanned, curley-haired, and smiles easily. He's comfortable, friendly, and easy to talk to. He genuinely wants to teach, to have as many people as possible learn what he and his guests have discovered.

He also wants to become governor of California. In the land of avocados, alfalfa sprouts, and jojoba, no one could represent the state of sunshine and opportunity better than Tony Hoffman.

Profile: Charles J. Givens, 45; Florida

Charles Givens is perhaps one of the more visable Get Rich teachers in circulation. Givens appears not only on his own television show, "A Millionaire's Secrets to Wealth," but numerous other broadcasts, including the NBC Network's "Today Show." Not only is Givens widely circulated, but his range of advice and knowledge covers many aspects of wealth.

Even the big networks actively recruit Givens for his style and no-nonsense expertise. The "Today Show" itself has had Givens appear six times since just last summer. He has also debated a "Money Magazine" senior reporter on television, discussing many of the Givens discoveries for making big money.

Many of the New Wealth advisors hail real estate as the best method for acquiring their fortunes. Givens understands real estate and has made his own fortune. But what good is financial independence unless you know how to manage it? No one can hang onto wealth without further understanding how to make that fortune work while you've got it. So, Givens understands not only how to make a fortune, but how to keep it, too.

Givens can show you how to make your fortune grow on its own through stocks, bonds, and annuities. And taxes? He can also show you how to save there, too. His combination of investment and tax-saving know-how has been widely accepted by thousands of people who want their own financial independence.

Since 1975, 110,000 people have joined the Charles J. Givens Foundation to get their share of the riches so many people deserve. The Givens Foundation, a non-profit company, has taken in more than $30 million, half of that revenue in 1985 alone. For the price of a life-time membership, $295 (payable by credit card), all participants in the Foundation receive a workbook, cassettes, a monthly newsletter, and a two-day workshop. Sales are expected to hit $20 million in 1986, Givens says. That ought to give you some idea of how successful you can be with a little knowledge from this man.

Givens himself is tall, tanned, and blond. He owns his own jet for travel purposes and sports a monogrammed luxury automobile when on the ground. He lives in a million dollar home built on a private lake in Florida, and earns $250,000 per year "on the side" from his teaching and appearances on behalf of the Foundation.

Givens' techniques include a deep understanding of motivational tools as well as personal finance savvy. If you want to learn how to deduct the price and operational expenses of a VCR player and camera from your taxes, Charles Givens knows how. Or maybe you want to find out how you can earn a 65 percent return on a simple IRA. Again, Givens knows how.

Having made his millions already, Givens says he continues to search for new "victories over poverty." On top of all he already knows about fortunes, finance, and hanging onto wealth, he is also a general partner in two real estate partnerships (minimum investments of $3,000) that are buying and developing income producing property in central Florida.

So, if you're looking for not only real estate investing advice, but also tips on how to hang on to that wealth with tax-saving tips and "money-making-money" inside knowledge, check out Charles Givens. He has helped over 100,000 people begin their journey on the rapid-paced road to riches. Thousands more are joining every week. A floodgate of new millionaires has been opened, and people "jump in" with television, Charles Givens, and "A MIllionaire's Secrets to Wealth."

Profile: Ed Beckley, 38; Iowa

How many people, millionaires even, pocketed $8 million last year, as pay, after all company expenses? Well, at least one man. That was Ed Beckley. The Beckley Group, based in the heartland of America (not a show business capital) had revenues in 1985 of $30 million. The company netted $10 million, $8 million of it going to Ed Beckley.

Figures like that kind of stagger the imagination. Yet some people find that kind of success fuels their motivation to go out and chase a dream of their own. Beckley is still a young man. He earned his first million dollars at an even younger age. These days, he shares his secrets of wealth.

10,000 people a week are now paying for Ed Beckley's secrets. Beckley himself pays half a million dollars a week for air-time on television, spreading the word. His show appears up to 800 times a week on 400 stations across the country. Show production costs can run as high as $15,000 to $30,000. In 1985, $30 million was paid to televise those Beckley secrets.

In return, Beckley sells his "No Money Down" home-study course for just $295. Another course, "The Credit Card Millionaire," costs $299. These tested secrets of Beckley's can pay for themselves with a single tip. After that, it's money in the bank.

So, what does Ed Beckley know? Beckley knows how to get real estate with no money down or through cash advances on ordinary credit cards. And he'll tell you, or anyone else who happens to tune in, just how it's done.

Beckley isn't shy about revealing his secrets and teaching others. On no less than three television shows, Ed Beckley can be seen on almost any cable channel, at any time of day, and on any given day of the week. His shows are: "The Millionaire Maker," "Fortune Formulas," and "Credit Card Millionaire."

The Beckley Group employs over 500 people to help those who study with him. The Beckley Group operates on $3 million in weekly revenues. How's that for financial know-how? Sales are expected to hit $150 million in 1986! In 1987, Beckley will establish a cable network devoted exclusively to fortune making and motivational programming. The new network will be called, naturally, "The Success Channel."

And this man knows about success. By the time Ed Beckley was 30 years old, he was a millionaire. It was at that time that he quit his job as a high school business teacher. He'd made so much money on the side in real estate around Quincy, California, he decided to move "back to the farm" and persue real estate investing full-time.

Beckley's investing organization, a partner, and their families, moved to Iowa, kids and all. After several years touring with a two-day, $445 seminar, Beckley wanted to settle down. A shop-by-mail, home-study course on the Beckley knowledge has resulted. And, it leaves him time to devote himself to his interests, the television shows, and sharing his knowledge with even more people - people who want to change their lives forever with a million dollars - or more!

Profile: Carleton Sheets, 46; Florida

While some people are merely interested in beginning a real estate investing career, and others have been at it for only a short while, Carleton Sheets has been making it work for him for over 15 years. Sheets is a millionaire, at least a couple of times over. He appears in national seminars and on television in over 40 cities around the country.

Ask the question: can a veteran investor and teacher make "it" work for an average American, anyone interested in producing income from, say, rental property?

Absolutely! Just look at what happened to a man named Ken Chlopecki. Fate - and an outsider's challenge - changed Chlopecki overnight. The challenge came from newspapers in Chicago, the Chicago Sun-Times, to be exact. In October of 1984, the Sun-Times printed a challenge directed to Carleton Sheets, a challenge that a single average American couldn't do what the successful investor knew was possible. And the challenge thought it would be tough: prove that in just one day, Sheets could successfully teach a novice to buy rental property for no money down that would produce a positive cash flow.

Sheets knew his experience and real estate knowledge could be taught. He knew that anyone could learn what he could teach. He accepted the challenge and in ONE DAY transformed ONE MAN. Chlopecki, 38, a machine shop inspector, spent one day with Carleton Sheets. Then, on his own, and OVERNIGHT, Chlopecki bought and began making rental income from a townhouse in nearby Bolingbrook, Illinois.

Well, Carleton Sheets hasn't heard from the Sun-Times since then, but the point was well proven: without using one's own money, residential property can be bought for no money down. One can own income producing real estate anywhere. The fact that these properties can also be sold at any time at great profits is another entire matter.

Perhaps you understand this already, perhaps you don't. If you watch Carleton Sheets on TV, you'll soon find out. Sheets appears on the Financial News Network (FNN), the Satelite Program Network (SPN), and other television stations all around the U.S. On a show titled "The Keys to Success," several very successful millionaires are interviewed by Art Fleming, host of the money-quiz show, "Jepordy."

Some people make it big in the cookie business, somebody else with the cosmetics industry. But when Sheets comes on, the viewer quickly realizes that Carleton Sheets has made his fortune - in Money! And, particularly, through real estate.

In an earlier life, Carleton Sheets was a salesman for an industrial packaging company. But that was seemingly another lifetime ago. Since 1970, Sheets has applied his unique knowledge about how money works - and how none of his own has to be used to make more of it. Using real estate is the perfect method for using other people's money to make even more money - for yourself.

As far as Carleton Sheets is concerned, he can make his knowledge work for anyone like it worked for Ken Chlopecki in a single day. Sheets spends what little spare time he has with the two-day seminars he offers around the country for $395. The traveling schedule takes time, but Sheets also produces a home-study course for the low price of $195. And, to further the teaching of the largest number of people possible, the FNN and SPN cable channels can let anyone hear what Carleton Sheets can teach.

Profile: Dave Del Dotto, 35; California

"Cash Flow is King," exclaims Dave Del Dotto. And this home-grown California boy ought to know. Del Dotto grossed over $7 million in 1985 as the middleman for many profitable deals. Real estate, cars, TV's, Del Dotto knows how to properly position himself. He knows how to buy at a fraction of any item's value and he quickly re-sells at full retail. The difference is money in the pocket, profit from cash flow.

Even when Dave Del Dotto was in his early 20's, he knew how to reach into the fast moving, deep rivers of cash flow and come up soaked with cash. He learned that key knowledge, alertness, and timing made all the difference in the world of money. While testing his instincts, Dave knew that luck had nothing to do with nothing - positioning was the key.

Positioning meant opening your eyes and ears. Positioning meant going right up to the right places, making sure to be there at the right time. Positioning meant obtaining property and merchandise at absolute bottom prices. The difference that positioning made was Profit.

Dave Del Dotto's many years of experience has resulted in an information system which he now passes on to America. Since 1984, Del Dotto has appeared on weekend television. Two cable channels carry his message:" Cash Flow Expo" is shown on cable's Black Entertainment Television on Saturdays from 3 p.m. to 4 p.m. "Second Cash Flow Expo" can be seen also on Saturdays from 9 a.m. to 10 a.m. over the USA Network.

Through television and a $298 home-study course, Del Dotto teaches high profit maneuvers to those new to making big money. Seminars and cassettes list numerous bargain locations and methods for buying distressed properties, foreclosures, and sell-off merchandise at government sales and auctions. Who wouldn't want a luxury car seized by customs agents and sold off for a fraction of its value at a sparsely attended auction?

This junior college drop-out hasn't done badly for himself. Del Dotto Enterprises in Modesto is located in the two-story Del Dotto Building. Dave has been dealing in real estate since 1974. In 1979 he also opened an office in nearby Sonora and sold houses, apartments, and office buildings. By 1982, Dave owned 25 houses, 20 apartment units, five office buildings and other properties in Modesto, Sonora, and vacation properties in Orlando, Florida.

In 1984, Dave became interested also in housing and other property foreclosures. This was at about the same time other people were telling Dave he should expand his lecture circuit to include teaching on television. Combined with his strategy of aiming his energy at sales, auctions, and notices of distressed property and merchandise, "Cash Flow is King" became his slogan.

Dave has expanded his interests to include a recording company and he has plans to produce a screenplay as well. Given his success in helping thousands of other people to make their fortunes with cash flow, Dave is looking forward to his next dream: a real estate brokerage firm with offices in 200 cities country-wide. Look for Dave Del Dotto on television. Your fortune may just be around the corner. Jump into the Cash Flow of TV advertising - you might just wind up soaking rich.

Profile: Wayne Phillips, 38; Arizona

Wayne Phillips doesn't sport a three-piece suit or believe in mincing words. "Why should I," he asks, when the average wage earner makes $8.77 an hour? If you think working for $8.77 will get what people want and deserve, you're mistaken."

What Wayne Phillips does believe is that a lot of money-making or fortune-hunting plans leave the average man in the cold, left at the gate, when it comes to high-ticket finance and wealth. That's why he teaches people that loans are available for property purchase and improvement, and rental incomes can not only pay off the loans, but also provide a handsome income.

"Most people don't have a thousand dollars lying around just waiting for a good piece of property to come along," Phillips points out. "That's why I believe everyone has a right to know about low-interest loans that are sponsored by agencies of the federal government. These loans are available to anyone who wants to own and fix up a rental property."

"What most people don't realize is that these loans exist. The rental income not only pays for the re-modeling of the property, but it also provides an income that pays off the loan. After that, there's income left over to provide a very good income for yourself."

Are you interested in creating wealth? Through a show on television by that very name, "Creating Wealth with Government Loans," you are already probably familiar with Wayne Phillips. Or you should be familiar wth him. His show appears ten times a week all across the country. Many stations carry "Creating Wealth with Government Loans" including the FNN, Lifetime, SPN, and USA networks.

One reason Wayne is on these shows is because he's aware of the many real estate oriented shows on TV. "But," he quickly adds, "I couldn't take advantage of people in distressed circumstances. I don't believe in prowling for 'motivated sellers,' people who are feeling desparate about family or financial hard times. That's why I prefer the less personal government loan system. I'm not taking advantage of anyone."

For a man living in a new spanish-style villa in Arizona, Phillips is quiet, but proud, about his own wealth. He'll concede only that his net worth does exceed one million dollars. Working in conjunction with the Federal Housing Authority and the Baltimore (Maryland) Department of Housing and Community Development, Phillips practices what he preaches. This former jazz drummer from Baltimore and his company, the Greater Baltimore Building Corporation, exists through the insured apartment loans, which in turn provide for rehabilitation projects.

Wayne and his family (wife Cathleen and daughter Nicole) have lived in the southwest for two years now. Although Wayne produces a one-day seminar for $295, he spends more of his time providing a greater learning potential through the print and TV media. A thorough understanding of Wayne's financial technique is taught through a home-study course, forthrightly named the "Super Bird Dog" course. Priced at $349.95, this course supplies a 310 page book and 17 cassettes. Also provided are detailed listings and successful procedures to obtain any of the hundreds of low interest housing loans that are available.

These laons will be guaranteed and insured by the government housing agencies. Wayne explains, "These government sponsored mortgages and housing rehabilitation loans are the fastest, safest, most profitable ways to a million dollars through real estate."

Chapter 2

I Made $400,000.00 The First Time Out. But, You Can Do Better!

Economic conditions and marketing techniques have recently reached a point where anyone - and I certainly mean you - can learn the inside secrets I used to make $400,000.00 dollars the first time out.

In this publication I'll show you how to utilize the power of television. I'll demonstrate to you that a $3 or $10 (cost) item (book or product) can be sold to hundreds of thousands of people for ten or twenty times what you paid for it. And, what's more, I'll take you step by step through the writing directing, and producing of your own commercial for about the price of a car payment.

I'll explain how an easily established ad agency of your own can get you immediate discounts on air-time. Or, if you prefer (and I like this part), how your ad can get air-time FREE at the TV station's insistence.

TV Stations need you more than you need them. I'll show you why. (But more about that latter.) Now I want to tell you that there's an whole new opportunity just waiting for you to step into.

In this publication, I'll lay out for you all the ingredients that go into making a commercial: the idea, the creation, the script writing, how to find a recording studio for your sound track, how to find a film company to get your commercial "in the can." I'll tell you exactly, in plain words, how to cut all the red tape - and reduce most of the costs.

Once you understand the first step, the second step, third step, and so on, you'll be able to produce a commercial for a product or book. You will film on a set or location, use live action or animation, and include inexpensive "purchased music rights" as a background. I'll familiarize you with marketing your commercial. You'll have your commercial on the air and pulling sales at a volume no other advertising medium can match.

I'll break down a sample commercial and show you its hidden moves. I will guide you practically second by second through the making of a commercial. And I won't leave you there. Marketing that commercial is your only real concern because the commercial takes care of selling the product. Once you have the commercial, you have more than a product to offer the public. You have a commercial that TV stations need, and I mean NEED.

I will show you the inside secrets of a TV station's business and its connection with advertising. The point is, the shoe is on the other foot in this business. They want your commercial, plain and simple. There's FREE time out there for your commercial, if you want to use it. And if you don't, then I'll show you how to buy air-time at a discount.

I'll take you inside the making of a deal for air-time, actual conversations between a TV sales department manager and myself.

Step by step, you can learn to cut costs and get big, big discounts on the best time allocations in the broadcast day.

No one has ever exposed the world of television advertising the way I'll do it for you right here. No one, I know of, has ever pointed the way to your first $400,000.00 dollars in TV advertising.

If you like to move fast, learn a few new tricks, and grab your share of the wealth, then let's go!

When I began successfully advertising on television, I knew nothing about the subject. I was a greenhorn. I wasn't nervous about the IDEA of advertising on television, just inexperienced. Yet, in a short while, I developed the ability to reach any market in the country and everyone with a TV set. My ads and the television stations do all the customer getting and order taking for me.

I'll run that by you again in a minute, but let me add to begin with that finding the right product wasn't a problem. Neither was dreaming up an ad. Producing my first commercial wasn't a big, mysterious affair. Putting the ad on film cost a couple of hundred bucks.

My inexperience with TV ads wasn't a strike against me. In fact, when I began, my inexperience probably helped me because I stuck to the basics which anyone can learn. I wasn't intimidated by TV, so I wasnt' scared away from trying. P.I. advertising (Free Advertising) led to bigger things, learning to set up my own in-house ad agency which allowed me to buy air time at substantial discounts. I now use various filming formats, too, but that came a few steps down the road.

You've heard that a little knowledge is sometimes a dangerous thing. If I'd thought I knew a few things when I began, I might have thought sure-winning products were hard to find. I might have thought I'd have to go to an agency to get an idea for my commercial. I would have paid high fees for a film company and huge air time costs.

If you think that's what you'd have to do, too, you're already scaring yourself out of TV advertising. No wonder. It seems unapproachable. When you look at it that way, it sounds like only big budgets can play.

Other people will tell you television advertising is too expensive. They say it's not geared to mail order. They call it unprofitable.

Frankly, there's not much to understand. I started with no previous exposure to it and I wasn't afraid of the subject. TV is simply a place to advertise. Realize that and you've discovered the first "secret." Don't let the apparent glamour of the tube blow it's image out of proportion. Don't make advertising out to be some great mystery.

If you examine television advertising, the mystery falls away and you can then produce a commercial. You can market on TV. But the producing and marketing of your commercial can never happen until you first de-mystify television advertising.

"Secret" *#1*

The first secret I'll tell you is that a TV ad is just a type of ad. Big deal, you say? Listen, there's no mystery. All ad types contain the same basic ingredients: name of product, its function or inherent value, it's price, and ordering instructions. So, stop letting the "romance" of the TV industry put you off.

A television ad is a sales offer with sound and motion. Yes, there are many styles for an ad. Styles can be learned. Styles exist that take very little to construct and film. I'll go into that for you. As long as you understand that television is a tool for advertising, you'll proceed quickly. Television is simply a way to reach people. It's a means of communicating.

"Secret" *#2*

The second secret is that producing a commercial for television is easier than you think. A TV viewer is a customer comfortably watching your ad. TV advertising has the power of sight and sound. The customers for a television ad are a very sizable group of easily accessible eyes and ears.

Producing your commercial is merely involved ad writing. How you can do it can easily be explained.

"Secret" *#3*

The real secret is that marketing your commercial doesn't even have to involve buying air time. Lots of the ads you see on TV don't have to cost a penny to get on the air. This "no investment" method of advertising is direct response advertising. It's also called "P.I." advertising—"per inquiry." P.I. advertising is not so much a way of buying air time. It's a way of offering a TV station good income with an ad. The rewards are yours.

Sure, you'll also learn to set up your own in-house ad agency like I did. If you buy air time, you can learn how to receive discounts off the standard rate charts. These charts will be us-

We've blown the lid off!

ed by the sales departments at television stations. The marketing inside knowledge I give you will enable you to choose between no-risk P.I.'ing or reaching big markets at special rates.

You can begin putting your commercials on TV as soon as you examine this high volume advertising medium. This I will do right along with you. You need to know how to produce your ad. This is not a stage of advertising that you have to turn over to someone else to accomplish. Why pay others to do what you can do for yourself? Why pay the high cost of an outside agency? I'll tell you how to get your ad in front of the cameras without yet having spent a penny.

And as for marketing your commercial, air time doesn't have to be bought. P.I. advertising can mean the ad pays for itself.

What all this boils down to is that advertising on television is as open to you as anything else. The easy part is creating the ad. The fun part is producing it. That leaves the exciting part: participating in the high volume market and sales of advertising on television.

Chapter Three
FREE Advertising.

"P.I. Advertising"

Any other way of selling products is just that, selling products. The many ways to sell just another product are all risky, but the truth is, most forms of mail order business are just plain lonely. I'll tell you why I say that. Does this sound like a lot of the standard experiences people have when trying to make money with a mail order business?

"Gee," says John Doe, new entrepreneur to mail order schemes. "I hope my product's a hot one"..."Gee, is the price OK?"..."Gee, are my costs high?"..."Gee, is this ad right? Is it too small?"..."Gee, look at those ad space costs! Is my ad in the right newspapers and magazines?"..."Gee, is the mailman coming?"... "Is this all?"..."Gee, what am I going to do with all this stuff?"

Boy! Talk about a lonely business! And no wonder! All this guy's offering is a product, good or bad, and while he's sticking it out there, the only thing in this with him is his crossed fingers.

You have something that this guy doesn't have. It's a cost free ingredient and it spells the difference between his lonely uncertainty and your certain low risk profiting. John Doe is trying to work with the print media and let's face it, people are reading less and less every year. But Mr. Doe is trying to work in partnership with the mail system. Well, now, that's good enough as a means of getting products shipped and having orders come in. But, frankly, there's really nothing in it for the U.S. Mail except some cost coverage (and we all know how much they're losing). Some partnership!

Now what if you had the same product, let's say an inexpensively bought excercise product, just right for a health conscious and excercise hobby-ist in America. Now, you know this quality product bought in bulk goes for peanuts. You know also that you could sell it at twice your cost or maybe even for three or four times your cost. Not a bad profit, right? Sure, according to "standard" mail order formulas.

You know something else, too, namely this: People love to make money. And there's an entire industry waiting for people like you, maybe, who can help them make the money they need to stay in business. What you do is this (and it's this move that sets you apart from John Doe): you make a commercial for your product. That commercial is going to go on the air. You're going to put it on the air as a P.I. advertising program.

You've got the product and the commercial. TV stations, have air space to sell. They have all sorts of costs in their business. There's programing to buy, there's their own programming to create and film, staffs to pay, technicians, electricity. How they get their revenue just like the print media, by selling ad space, but TV stations have air time, not ad space. They've got to break for at least two minutes, or more, periodically to run ads to pay for all their operational costs. They need the revenue.

Their biggest headaches are "unasked for time-slots," ... unsold air time, and the advertiser that cancels at the last minute. Some stations even go looking for P.I. programs when money's tight.

To Change the subject for a second let me tell you about Newspapers & Magazines. When you have a product and need to advertise it, the print media is the first place most people go. You call them up and tell them you want to place a full page ad in their magazine. Their sales department probably couldn't care less from the sound in their voice. "OK," they say, "What size, please...etc, etc." And then you pay for that ad space.

Most so called "authorities" on doing mail order business will tell you that's a cost you can't avoid. Wrong! I am going to show you how to avoid those costs.

On the other hand, when you have a TV commercial "in-the-can" for a product and you call a TV station, the tone of the whole transaction changes. You are offering a P.I. deal so they can make money from the station's dead air time. In order to fill this dead air time they sometimes use a public service announcement, or maybe they'd run something about an upcoming program or plug their station. You've seen "ads" like this when stations take a break. That was unsold air time. They didn't make a dime.

So, when you call up and offer a P.I. deal, the next thing you know, you have a partner with a powerful media at your disposal. A "P.I. deal" is loaded with incentive for the TV station and they will want to work with you.

All of a sudden, you're not lonely like the John Doe Magazine advertiser, with no money in his pocket for advertising. The main difference between you and John Doe is that he has just a product to sell. You, on the other hand, have a commercial to sell that will make money for the TV station and you, too. You're selling the P.I. offer, not just a product (your commercial does that).

TEAMWORK WINS!

Chapter Four
How To Make FREE Advertising Work For You

Few insiders are going to give you this knowledge. Few advertisers even have this knowledge. It's P.I. advertising. That's short for Per Inquiry and it can't lose. When you strike a P.I. arrangement with a television station, they get a percentage of the retail price of your product. There are no other charges.

Once you have your commercial "in hand," you call a television station. You'll want to ask them for the sales department. Ask then for the person at the station who handles P.I. advertising programs. If the station doesn't know who does that, ask for the general sales manager. Tell him you have a commercial and tell him it's available as a P.I. program for the station. They'll want to know what the product is, so here's your cue to sell that product. *NOTE: See Chapter Five.* Important: sell the commercial. Tell him how long it runs. Is it a :60 or a two minute ad? How's it look? Tell him it's all set, the tag is on the film. Tell him what the selling price is. Then tell him what percentage your P.I. deal will pay the station.

Now, the percentage could vary. Some people may play it real safe. They don't want to risk having their P.I. deal rejected. They might offer 50%. Experience may later teach you that 50% is pretty high. On the other hand, skating by with an offer of 20% takes some guts. At least guts and a very fine commercial. All things equal, the 30-35% range should suit most television stations.

Now, sometimes you'll need that extra push. Either you or the TV sales department may need a little confidence to push the P.I. deal through. So 50% may sway the station for you when you're new to P.I.'ing. After the higher percentages have worked for you with the first dozen stations, you'll feel more comfortable. You'll gain the savy and confidence for offering the lower percentages.

Later it won't make much difference. You should have the following three things going for you: the station likes P.I.'ing and recognizes a money-making opportunity; your commercial adheres to the general standards of broadcasting and isn't "chancey" for the station; and your rapport with the sales manager is excellent. Once you can briefly establish these factors in your phone call, a P.I. arrangement can be made.

The rapport you have with the sales manager is mostly in your hands. That rapport will be gained the more the sales manager experiences dealing with you. Demonstrate that you can deliver the goods. And always deliver what you promise. Stay in frequent contact with the stations. Of course, while gaining this rapport, don't be a pain. You're not the only person offering a deal. There are other advertisers out there, other callers. So don't just call to shoot the breeze. Be friendly, but be business-like about your calls. Remember: P.I. advertising is a mutual favor.

A two-way street is a good viewpoint. Income may be a little slow at the station. Unsold time is sometimes a fact of life for small stations. A P.I. deal can keep them alive like a money transfusion. Things can get to the point where *you* get the calls. *They'll* be calling *you* to see if you have any P.I. deals to help them out of a slump.

These inner-workings between a P.I. advertiser and a television station can be revealing. What follows is the behind the scenes selling of a P.I. deal. Pay attention. The odds are extremely good that you can get your product and a P.I. deal on TV. Here's what my phone call to a station sounds like when I'm putting together a P.I. program:

P.I. PHONE CONVERSATION FOLLOWS:
STATION OPERATOR: KDTT-TV, May I help you?
   : Yes, good morning! Would you please tell me who handles P.I. advertising at KDTT-TV?
OPERATOR: "Sir, I don't know who that would be."
   : "Well, that's OK. Would you please connect me with your station's sales department then?"

SALES DEPARTMENT PERSON: "Sales..."
: "Hello. Who handles P.I. advertising there?"
SALES: "Hmmm..."
: "Don't know? That's OK. Could I please speak to your sales manager then? What's his name?"
SALES: "Dick Schorter."
: "Thanks very much."
DICK: "This is Dick Schorter. May I help you?"
: "Hi! Yes you can. How are you today?"
DICK: "Pretty good. You, too?"
: "Oh, yes, feeling fine. Thanks for asking. Listen, Dick, the reason I'm calling you is to make an offer. I've got a commercial for a (coin sorter) that's doing really well for me. I thought I'd call you and see if its sales might be of interest to you."
DICK: "Well, tell me a little bit about it. We're pretty tight with our time right now."
: "I understand. It's a great little product that the viewers can't resist. Some of the stations around here are having a great draw with it, in fact, everywhere I've placed it, sales have been really high. It's a new product that most people haven't seen before. I've got two models in the ad, of course. It's a winner, not a filler."
DICK: "Nice package. What's the cost?"
: "$14.95 for the super model, $9.95 for the standard."
DICK: "What's the pay-out?"
: "$2.50, and $4.50 pretty nice, huh?"
DICK: "Yeah."
: "I've got all the coin sorters in stock, do all the work here and turn the whole thing around the same day we get the orders. I haven't had a customer problem yet with this one. I just don't work any other way."
DICK: "Well, I don't have any two-minute slots open right now..."
: "Like I said, this is a :60. We specialize in :60's. These spots slip right in. We know your time is not all that loose."
DICK: "Well, what about back-ups? Gotta have some back-ups just in case some customer hangs their complaint on us."
: "Won't happen here, Dick, sure we've got back-ups. I can send you six of each coin sorter to cover you, but like I

said, we ship out the same day, so take the back-ups anyway, but there won't be any problems."

DICK: "OK,   , send the sixes and a dub out right away. Got the tag?"

: "Oh, yeah, here's the simple audio: have your announcer use the end of the music as his cue, and he says: "Here's how to order: Send $14.95 for the super coin sorter, $9.95 for the standard model, to "Coin Sorter"—say, what's your box number, Dick?"

DICK: "98."

: "Right. 'Coin Sorter' Box 98, Pittsburgh, Pa." That's your audio for the tag and here's the video: make your slide, "$14.95 for super" space $9.95 for standard"—right across the screen top. Slide 'Coin Sorter' center, mid-screen, and that's it!"

DICK: "OK. Got it."

: "Terrific! Listen, I'll have everything out today. I'll give you a call after that to see how the dub's doing with you, check the broadcast date, so forth. Thanks for the chat. I want you to have a real good day down there today, Dick, take care."

DICK: "OK, say, thanks for calling, talk to you."

A CLOSER LOOK AT THE CONVERSATION

OK, deal's done. Plain, simple, to the point, no great time loss. That's it. But let me tell you, a lot was going on there, more than either of us let on, but that's business. Let me show you what was happening here. The whole conversation was kept to the point, as you can see. When the sales manager needed the sell, I sold. When all he needed was a short answer to a short question, that's what I gave him. Most of all, we both kept the conversation light, friendly, but not too personal or too business like. But be loose or he'll turn you off with a very business-like "No thank you, goodbye."

Now, I got through to the person I needed to talk to, but I first asked to speak with someone who handles P.I.'ing at the station. It will happen, from time to time, that an operator or even the sales department won't know what you're talking about. I didn't have to tell Dick I had a P.I. offer, he'd been able to tell that just by listening. As for the other people, it's not that they never heard of P.I. advertising. They just don't know it by that name. Most people do, though. More importantly, by using the term 'P.I.' I got right through. I didn't have to use some long winded explanation of why I was calling. An operator doesn't want to hear the pitch, she just wants to move the call right along. I didn't stop and try to educate her either. I just need her to do her job and put someone on the line.

As soon as he said it sounded pretty good, I assured him I could deliver the goods, right down to 'back-ups' and complete tag instructions. At this point in the conversation, after basic acceptance, I don't want to bring up anything that might throw water on the deal. I made the rest of the deal flow like a river, easy and simple. I assured him of my professionalism and my ability to make the deal work for both of us. That's what a sales department wants to hear.

See? Frankly, it's easy. You go from product to TV advertising. For the small or big operator, it's easy. You might begin with small stations. The large network air-time may not always take a P.I. deal. First you learn the ropes, pay your dues, with lots of stations. You'll be gaining real experience all the way. You'll be gaining that "touch" for timing and an ease dealing with air-time salespeople.

The commercial markets the product. You market the commercial. Pay attention to that dinstinction. To more fully understand the difference, examine the following tips. If you keep this information in the back of your mind, the packaging of a P.I. program can't miss.

FACT: When you're talking to a sales manager at a TV station, he'll sound interested. You're offering revenue. He likes the P.I. arrangement. Your prospects seem bright, but you want to help him make up his mind.

FACT: You know ahead of time that a station's unsold time is lost revenue. It's gone money. Bear this in mind for a little extra amunition when dealing, but just don't mention it out loud. The print media never loads up their pages with filler public service announcements. A TV station, for many reasons, has "empty pages" and "has to" fill their breaks while on the air. Few stations will always turn down P.I. deals.

Nearly all small to medium size stations periodically run "slow." You can tap the near-regular frequency and availability of no cost/low cost air time. For months at a time your commercial can "star burst" all around the country. And that's just one commercial plus one P.I. program.

Let me help you jump ahead with this idea. A quality, successful P.I. advertising program is like a level entry. Things can grow vertically very quickly. When you're continuously registered with numerous stations locally, national organizations can by then be handling your commercial. You can see the spread. Between the P.I. experience and discounted air time, a wide range of reduced rates are at your disposal. I mean, right up to Super Bowl air time, a sudden unsold time slot went for 75 percent off! A sales manager had to quickly call a P.I.'er for a commercial that made them both money!

Chapter Five

P.I. Advertising Can Make You A Fortune. But, Sometimes You're Better Off Using Your In-House Ad Agency.

Per inquiry advertising is a money-making proposition for the television station. Remember, they're in the business of selling air time to advertisers. There are many levels of air time and many prices for advertisers. The sales department of a television station works night and day soliciting advertisers and responding to advertisers needs, usually well inadvance of air time. Fortunately for you they don't always manage to sell all their time or they may have cancellations that ruin their well laid plans for filling all the 2:00 breaks throughout the day. Of course the station could always fill the blank time with public service announcements and the like, but they would prefer to run a PI ad that translates to revenue.

PI advertisements involve products selling for approximately twice their usual selling price. The advertiser, in exchange for air time, gives anywhere from 25-50% of proceeds from sales to the television station. So, not only is television advertising a lucrataive tool for the advertiser, it can make pretty good money for the station, too. The willingness of a station to do PI business depends on many factors, primarily the availability of unsold time. PI advertisers are sometimes lined up, like jets in a holding pattern over a busy airport, each waiting to be dropped in at the earliest opportunity. On that "tag" at the end of your commercial, the station announcer will give a repetition of your product name, the price, and usually a mailing address for the station. A record of responses to your ad will be tallied and the percentage of proceeds that goes to the station will be your cost of doing business on TV.

A station won't hear of doing PI business when times are good, except possibly for the finest, most fantastic product ever going. But try again and again. Lean days for them is a gold mine for you. TV stations always have to sell ad time. They can't shrink their broadcast days like a magazine or newspaper shrinks their pages to compress their size to fit fewer advertisers. They can't lengthen their programs either. They have to break for at least two minutes and they have to fill that space. From an advertising agency you can get the TV Standard Rate and Data Book. Call an agency and ask for old ones. Study them, skipping large city stations and the networks. You'll be able to tell who does PI advertising, who doesn't, or who does periodically (or seasonally). If you solicit the business of a distant station, write letters to your prospects extolling the virtues of your product, your ability to ship orders promptly, etc. Follow up with phone calls. One acceptance anywhere will influence other stations in considering a PI basis relationship.

Your direct response advertisement's worth to the television station can quickly be assessed by the sales department. P.I. advertising is a very, very good money making arrangement for them. They'll drop your one or two minute commercial in at timeslots that meet their needs (an "R.O.S."—run-of-station—schedule) in cases where unfilled or cancelled time exists. You do not have the ability to control air time, but the station may see high returns for themselves and run your ad five times in an hour or simply once a day on several days in the month. When the commercial makes money for them, they'll run it "whenever." A good commercial is a faucet of money for both of you.

The station receives all mail or phone requests and takes in all receipts. On a regular basis, all orders will be handed over to you for shipping and the station will send you the agreed upon portion of the proceeds. So, imagine the $5 cost item advertised on a P.I. basis for $35 on television. Even a 40% P.I. fee to the station is a *net* to you of $18 per item. Your profits leap by the 10's of thousands with advertising. Better buying of goods and higher selling prices on the P.I. television ad increase profits for both you and the television station. The relationship between advertiser and the television

medium is one of mutual gain and no risk or huge investing. Now you know.

So now you know that advertising on television was made for you. The medium exists for you. In the world of mail order and television, some basic guidelines should be followed for testing and marketing TV advertising:

Guideline #1—When I run one ad, just once, for a market testing, the results will tell me enough to be 85% sure if the product's right or wrong. If I'm still uncertain for whatever reason, or if the results were unfavorable, I may run the ad once more. Who knows, maybe the weather was against me (another station drew the viewers)? But if results are still unfavorable, I may throw the product out and begin again. Actually, more likely as not, I'll "shelve" the ad for awhile. Since timing can be everything, its day will come and the commercial will win for me yet.

Guideline #2—Always try to find air time that is very late at night. The same can be said for very early in the morning. People after midnight and early in the morning are your best audience. At any rate, the last hours of the day and the wee-hours of the morning are hours that are the best for ad testing. If you want reliable results.

Additionally, don't buy package deals when looking for air-time. Never buy a full week or two if you're testing. There are a few, just a few, unscrupulous TV sales managers out there. You might wind up buying a dozen bad time-slots for many more dollars than you'd even pay for one bad time-slot. Later, if and when you know the sales manager better, package deals can be put together that you'll both benefit from. A three-day schedule would be plenty if you're testing.

Guideline #3—There's nothing wrong with being a beginner at all this. We were all beginners at one time or another, believe me. The crime, though, is sounding like a beginner. Coming across like a greenhorn can cost you credibility. I'm not saying that a newcomer can't get in the door. I'm saying that if you sound like you don't know what you're doing, just getting ear-time will be difficult. If you have hesitancy in your voice or if you sound unsure while you tell the sales manager how much good you can do for him, that ear-time may be short. Study the phone conversations I've written for you. Trust in the sales manager's instincts for making money. Be comfortable. Put yourself in the other guy's shoes. Remember: you're not selling your product to a customer, you're offering a P.I. deal for the station.

Guideline #4—The total return from the run of your commercial is your gross retail. As for pricing, the acceptable formula is that the price of the product, what you pay for it, should be one-fifth of the selling price. Now, these are *minimal* formulas. Many other factors in your commercial's costs will vary. And when you're P.I.'ing, there are some ingredients you can control very handsomely. The costs of producing your commercial can be minimized. A P.I. deal covers its air-time costs. And some paid time, discounted "sudden loss" revenue, can be picked up for peanuts. Just make sure in your price formula you take the basics into account.

Guide #5—This one's simple: even if your ad has been successfully tested, keep testing. A product's "time" comes and goes at no man's discretion. Maybe the product did well in one section in the country and you want to try another. Maybe a station calls you, looking for a P.I., and he wants one run before. Don't assume prevailing winds will carry you. Use your instincts. Base your decisions on frequent testing and fresh test results.

Guideline #6——Since you already know to completely trust the late, late hours, or early morning hours, when *do* you want to get air-time? When you're buying air-time for direct response advertising, 3:00-7:00 p.m. Sunday Afternoon is best. Many studies have demonstrated this fact. Now, I'm not saying you'll always run into the availability of this time period. And, when you're P.I.'ing, your pick of the air-time is a non-issue. But keep Sunday in mind. Also, and this may seem too basic to mention, but it's not: always *ask* for the direct response advertising rates. Unless you ask, standard rates will not be offered. That's how simple that is.

Guideline #7—Just about *any* time on the weekends can be a good time for you. During any hour of Saturday, even of course Sunday, can work nicely. People's pattern of life are very different on weekends compared to the work week. Obviously, the dead of night after midnight Saturday is great, but Sunday a.m. can't be beat, particularly if your ad is opposite religious programming. Think about it.

Guideline #8—When you're testing TV ads, always provide that tag for ordering: an address to buy from and an 800 number for ordering. Within a half hour of your commercial's run, you have a measurement of 75% of the total response you will receive. This will give you a pretty accurate idea of how well you'll do with that one ad. This will also give you a good measuring stick for testing that ad in other markets, too. Don't even start trying to count all your chickens by tabulating the mailed in responses. That takes time and meanwhile you're still waiting to decide how well the ad is going to do. Let the mail response be a cushion, the "extra" cream on top of test results.

Guideline #9—Unless you've got very good reasons, *never* use a small answering service for your 800 number. Not even if they're close, not if your brother in law owns the service. What you're paying them for is service and they haven't got what it takes to handle mail order responses. They're probably not familiar with taking orders, just names, numbers and messages. Plus, they don't have the manpower to handle a lot of calls. You'd never know how well you could have done with a product if an under-staffed answering service just took the phones off the hook. I always try to get a service that's used to mail order phone action. Look for a service that has 40 or 50 operator in service. And test them. After your ad has run, phone the service. If you get too many rings, they didn't have enough operators to handle the calls. In your test results, the service will tell you they got a low response. And, what if you get a busy signal? Well, your ad may be a huge success, but also, another direct mail offer may have run at the same time. If that happened, you'll wind up with a low response. But if the line stays busy, and you get a low response figure from the service, chances are they just took the phones off the hook. So, a mail response phone service has to be chosen wisely and tested often. They can bankrupt you quicker than selling ear-muffs in Hawaii. Here's two large professional 800 phone service companies I use and can recommend:

National Switchboard
P.O. Box 32069
Phoenix, AZ 85064
1-800-262-5389

Nice Corporation
4357 South Airport Plaza
Ogden, Utah 84405
1-800-453-9000

GUARANTEED
(Results)

Chapter Six

Discounts, Means Money In Your Pocket. Use Your In-House Agency.

Cheap air-time isn't just hanging out on the trees, there for the picking. There'd be no Standard Rate and Data books if that was so. However, discounted time is closer at hand than you might imagine. It's still not out on the tree limb, but it is hidden in the bushes. You just need to know where to look and how to pick it up. A couple of simple moves on your part will practically put less expensive time right in your hands.

If you're P.I.'ing, there aren't any discounts offered or possible in the first place because the ad pays for it's own time. The station runs the ad with their own left-over or suddenly unsold time and makes you both money. But in paid-for direct mail response rates, any discount you can get is money in the pocket.

The first thing you'll be glad to learn is that direct response rates are lower, much less lower, than regular rates. Direct response rates are not in print on a rate chart somewhere. These rates may also seem to vary from call to call, sales manager to sales manager These rates won't be found on a card they can send you. Oh, they have a standard rate chart they'll send if you ask them to, and these rates will be what they're willing to sell their advertising space for to national companies.

Here's where special rates comes into play. You can buy space locally for less money than I can. Since I'm coming in from the outside, I can't get the most elementary discount of them all, the discount offered local companies. It's a simple fact of life that advertisers in your area are better served by your local advertising media. They know where their bread is buttered and they're anxious to give you, the local company, the best service they can. They want you as a steady account and the local advertisers rates—less expensive space than they'll offer me (the out-of-towner)—are one way they make it easy on you.

Here's another plus: the advertising media is not only interested in having you, the local advertiser, do business with them. They are also interested in your potential customers being happy they heard about your ad. If you can just tell the advertiser that you have a local address where customers can be served, special direct response advertising rates will more likely be offered. They just want to be sure you aren't a fly-by-night outfit from nowhere. Now me? I suppose I could call up an advertiser in a city where my Uncle Joe lives and give them his address, but Uncle Joe might not be thrilled to take all my customers' calls. This is just another way of saying that some of the best discounted direct mail response rates might be right in your own backyard. The game rules are in your favor.

The third kind of discount is, in some ways, the special yet easy way to get a hefty discount on ad rates. Even easier than setting up for business, you can set up "D/B/A"—"doing business as"—an in-house ad agency status. Advertising agencies can get a quick 15% discount on all advertising. They simply pocket that discount as part of their profit. If you place your ads through an agency, you're already paying 15% more than you need to. Setting up your own in house ad agency will allow you to pocket that 15% for yourself. The same way that some company owners set up shop "T/A"— "trading as" (instead of incorporating), you can set up your own agency D/B/A. This agency is simply a subsidiary of your business. No other requirements for acting as your own agency really exist. Acting as your own advertising agent, the agreed upon advertising rate will automatically run 15% less. $200 worth of advertising suddenly becomes only $170. The extra money gets credited to your own agency. Now, there are some instances where this won't happen, but you can learn about those ahead of time.

First, you won't be getting additional discounts when you run a P.I. deal. That should be obvious by now. Since P.I.'ing costs you no money for ad time or ad space, what's to discount? Referring back to Guideline #3, don't wind up sounding like a greenhorn by stroking a P.I. deal and then asking how much discount you're going to get. Nothing discounted off nothing is just that, nothing.

Secondly, a few hard-liners may be out there when you try to get a discount for yourself just because you have an in-house advertising agency. Your company is the only account your agency has. You may not have a long line of established credit, they'll say. If your advertiser is having a tough day at the office, he may refuse the 15% discount and the credit. Actually, such is rarely the case. When I first began requesting discounts on my advertising on the basis of having my own in-house agency, I was very, very rarely turned down. Some of them are just interested in getting paid, naturally, so be respectful of their sensitivities. Maybe they never heard of you before, or you're just starting out. Some advertisers may even ask for a fraction of payment in advance, that's OK. You're by now talking about local rates, not national rates, and you've already gotten another 15% off at agency rates. Also, direct response rates are the subject, not regular rates, so a little pre-payment isn't going to amount to much.

Naturally, you're interested in hearing about a few more little crumbs, so pay attention when you're offered "2-10-30" arrangements. When you hear that, you're being offered an additional discount, on top of everything else, of another 2%. Your net billing will run this extra 2% less if you pay within 10 days of the normal 30-day billing period This extra discount is off the net billing. The figure arrived at after your 15% agency commission is deducted. It adds up. The sharp operator will get this little extra whenever he can.

So, you see, discounts on ad space are there if you know where to look and how to pick it up. A number of things can work in your favor when you go about it the right way. I'll cover super discounts for television advertising in a bit, but right here you can see that discounting on advertising space is there for the picking when you know what to do. With direct resonse rates, the space is cheaper. And, as a local advertiser, those rates you get close to home are better than I can get as an out-of-towner. Add to that the 15% you can shave off your low, local direct response rates by stating that you have your own in-house D/B/A advertising agency. And, to top it all off, get those costs down to the bone with the extra 2% whenever you can and whenever its offered.

TV Advertising at a Discount

How much of a discount can you expect to get on TV advertising? There's less magic to it than you probably think. Let me give you just one of my recent experiences as an example. Just a short while ago, I ran a spot in an late evening time-slot. I paid about $200 for one minute of ad time. And I know for a fact that just one minute before my commerical, another advertiser paid $1,000 for the same one minute airspace! And he was a local retailer!

So what did I know that the other guy obviously didn't know? What did I do differently than him? Not all that much. I wound up with two spots in a couple of nights that ran around $500 for both commericals and I made, net, after all expenses, around $3,000. And I could do it night and day if I wanted.

You've got to remember, and I'll say it again and again, air space is raw revenue potential to a TV station. They can't let that air time go unsold. Sure, they can fill it in with station promotions or public service announcements, but that doesn't put a cent in their pockets. And once the unsold air time is past, it's like money gone. They can't make it up, they can't just charge the next guy twice to make up for the lost time.

Now, there are at least a couple of ways you can take advantage of this lost time-lost revenue fact of life that TV stations have to live with. And there are people who will have different points of argument over this, and that's the P.I. route vs. buying time. Time at a discount aside, P.I.'ing is open to anyone who wants to quickly learn the ropes, make great money, and go about TV advertising with the least risk. P.I.'ing with several stations to start with will get you the experience you need to cut the sharpest deals and maximize your profits. But in a little while, you'll be ready for the really profitable end of the business: paid time!

Now, I can show you how to be sharp when buying time, but before I do that, let's examine the short-cut to paid time. You have a couple of choices here and either one will be worth its weight in gold. Also, in both cases, you pass right by the P.I. end of direct response advertising.

Number one: you can employ a national agency, for a percentage, to get your direct response ad on the air. These guys are in the business to help everyone. A top rated agency has lists and lists of TV stations doing direct response advertising year in and year out. They keep in touch with the stations and offer a variety of direct response ads all the time. Some of the biggest agencies do their job so well that the TV stations call them, looking for a quick money-raising commercial. I can tell you about that later, but, if you're smart, you'll remember the 15% an agency gets for placing an ad. And you probably also realize you can do it for yourself.

This is one area where you can't let the energies slack. You may have to live with your telephone and get to know some stations like a cousin. Once you've made yourself known in the direct response mailing world, directly buying discounted air time can practically walk in the door.

Chapter Seven

How To Purchase Discounted Air-Time.

I just got off the phone this morning after talking with a TV sales department head. And, like the P.I. deal arrangement quoted earlier, I'll let you in on how the conservation went:

Discounted Air-Time Purchase Conversation Follows:
RECEPTIONIST: "WYYY, Channel 2..."
Steven: "Good afternoon. Would you please tell me who is your TV sales Manager?"
RECEPTIONIST: "Yes, that's Gary Wineman."
Steven: "Thank you. Could I speak to him please?"
SECRETARY: "Mr. Wineman's office, may I help you?"
Steven: "Yes, please, I'd like to speak to Gary, is he in now?"
SECRETARY: "Yes, he's in. Who's calling please?"
Steven: "This is Steven Houseman from San Francisco."
SECRETARY: "One moment, please."
GARY: "Hello, Gary Wineman."
Steven: "Hi, Gary, this is Steven Houseman from XYZ Marketing in San Francisco. I hope everything's going well for you today."
GARY: "Hi, how are you? Things have been a little crazy. What can I do for you?"
Steven: "Right to the point, I like that. Gary, the reason I'm calling you is we're interested in your market up there. We're beginning to come into the area with a direct-response product and maybe when your time is a little loose, we can both make a few bucks."
GARY: "Well, that's what I'm here for. What do you need?"
Steven: "I'm mostly interested in selective spot-buying. But if you've got a super deal I can't turn down, I'll listen. Other-

wise I'm not interested in anything packaged."
GARY: "Maybe I've got something for you."
Steven "OK, shoot, I'm listening."
GARY: "What have you got, a :60?"
Steven: "Right."
GARY: "OK! One of our packages always has a hit with direct-response buyers."
Steven "Tell me about it."
GARY: "We put you into the best times that come up, 20 spots, $800, R.O.S., and let me add..."
Steven: "Whoa, Gary whoa! I don't mean to cut you off, I apologize, but I don't want to waste your time. Look, I said selective time. I already know what I need. You have the Arbitron handy? How many households have you got 7:15 to 7:30 p.m. on Wednesdays?"
GARY: "Oh, well, let me see...324,000."
Steven "Uh-huh...what's that? News?"
GARY: "Right—for a minute? $1250."
Steven: "News?...hmmm...no, I'd never fit in there. What have you got at 7:45 p.m.?"
GARY: "Gameshow—169,000 households."
Steven: "Well, that sound pretty good. What's the minute go for?"
GARY: "$800."
Steven: "Wow! Hey! I'm a direct-response dealer. I can't go $800."
GARY: "What can I say. I'm reading the rate chart."
Steven: "Well, I don't want rate chart figures, I want direct-response rates. What can you really do for me?"
GARY: "Listen, how much can you go for the spot?"
Steven: "I'm allowed a buck per thousand households."
GARY: "The best I can do is $425."
Steven: "Well, I can't handle that. Across the street my buck per thousand was plenty. And I already know yours is a great market, that's why I'm calling you."
GARY: "OK, OK. $350, that's to the bone."
Steven: "Hey, thanks, but I can't do it. Listen, I've got a standard item here. You might lose some time some day, you want to sell the time and I want to buy some time. I know you've come down for me. Tell you what. Give me four of

HERE'S THE LATEST!

those spots for $200, I'll send it out right now. Put them in anywhere Monday through Friday. I'll come back and buy everything in those slots for three months, that is, if it sells. What do you say?"
GARY: "Well, that would be OK I guess..."
Steven: "Of course, it is. Great. Let's get clear on things. You know I can't pay more than allowed, so if things don't fly right away, you've got to pull it."
GARY: "That wouldn't be a problem. Off on a day's notice."
Steven: "Fine, fine, just needed to hear that. I'll come back for time as soon as this sells, but I can't get stuck for a loose "one or two week" kind of deal.
GARY: "I understand."
Steven: "I knew you would. Look, I'll have the dub and tag instructions out to you right away. Give you a call in a couple of days to see what you need. OK?"
GARY: "All right, talk to you again."
Steven: "Right, Gary, and thanks, call you soon."

Analysis of Conversation

Right away, before really looking at what went on in this conversation, look what happened. We started talking about a one minute time-slot for $1250 and I wound up with four one-minute spots each for only $200. That's the kind of discount advertising I'm talking about when I say time can be cheap! That's not even half the money someone else might have paid if they didn't go about it right. In fact, that's more than 90% off the higher priced spot we began talking about! Doesn't happen? Don't fool yourself.

Now, think about the differences between this conversation in which I bought air-time at a discount and the conversation involving a P.I. deal. But there were some similarities. Because I wanted to get right past the open door, I didn't waste time chatting with the secretary. I gave her my name and asked for someone in particular. I simply put myself in her shoes. Knowing it's her job to get names and give answers to questions, I didn't give her a hard time. Being brief, to the point, and businesslike usually pays off with those who first take your call.

And when I got the sales manager, I didn't rush him with a quick line of hard-sell. While people don't want their time wasted on the phone, they can appreciate a little chatter when they first pick up the phone. Even the busiest people like a little break that a phone call gives them. So, I asked how he was doing, even talked about the weather. When we were both comfortable after brief small talk, I got down to business. Even then, though, I didn't come right out and tell him I wanted to buy broadcast time, I just said I was "interested" in his market. Then I told him what I had and I slanted the information to let him know what he stood to gain from my offer.

I first asked him about the 7:15 p.m. time slot. I knew full well it was a news slot and that the Arbitron ratings were high. I wasn't interested in such a high cost time-slot, but the chance to get $1250 wetted the sales manager's interest in me. When I turned down the package deal of 20 spots, I didn't say the price was high, I just said I didn't want random time. I not only got selective in my time-slot wishes, but I also dragged the Arbitron book in there to show him I was talking households, not just any market. The 'per-household' figures I was going to use would later be the brick wall for what I could pay.

Even by the time we settled in on a cheaper time-slot, the figure came way down from his rate chart prices, $800 down to $425, then down to $350. I never said he didn't have room to move, he did it for me. The final move involved plain old simplicity, throwing out the $350 figure, stating what I expected for it, and that the money would go out right away. I simply said that I'd be back to buy more if the item sold well. The sales manager knew he'd have a chance to renegotiate rates with me. It was now in his interest, potentially, to go along with the sale of just four spots.

What I am attempting to do the whole time is control the flow of the conversation. I wanted to keep each ball coming right back to my court. I first put him at ease. I gave him a few moments to ease up and take his mind off whatever my call had interrupted. Next I told him who I am in the way of a direct response advertiser and that I had something for him. So, this is the way a beginner might go about it. Listen to how it goes when you've done business for awhile:

2nd Conversation follows:

Steven: "Hello, Gary? This is Steven Houseman, San Francisco. How's everything with you these days? Hey, that's good to hear. Gary, I've called to see what you can do for me during your afternoon schedules, any time in the week, say, 1 to 4 p.m.... Uh-Huh. By the way, how about your weekend scheduling? Sounds good. Tell you what, let me have two spots during the afternoon movies, Saturday and Sunday..."

The rest of our phone call is spent on pleasantries once we have business out of the way. First I'm offered a to-the-bone rate for weekday afternoon time slots. Naturally he'd like to sell a week's worth. Actually, I'm after the weekends. They're not only really good for the direct-response market, but they're cheaper than the weekdays. And, like I've said, once people are acquainted with you, business can be conducted smoothly and with mutual understanding.

So, things really do run smoothly after you've been at it for a little while. You can sell your products at first without many problems and without up-front investments. Buying up front is an invaluable way to get your feet wet, learn the ropes, test the angles, and begin to make yourself known in the country. You'll have a handle on the task and be able to improve the odds of your success tremendously. Your familiarity with the media will be your handiest tool when it comes to maximizing your profits. You'll have a money-making product which eventually you'll want to buy time for. You'll want to buy it at a large discount and won't need to throw any percentages to the station when you own your own time.

All this just goes to show you that not all time-buying deals are cut and dried. There *is* room for negotiation. But the real meat of this time-buying market is *what* you are buying. There's plain air-time and there's quality air-time. When you're P.I.'ing, air-time is air-time. Sure, the station wantsto make money with your P.I. deal. Just where the unsold time exists is another matter all together. When you *pay* for air-time, the whole point is either you get lucky with suddenly unsold time or you want to control when your ad is aired.

Some stations pull viewers better than others. Some shows continuously draw a bigger audience than others. Some time slots are best all around. Naturally, you want to have as many of these pluses going for you as possible. With a little homework, you can know ahead of time what a time-slot is going to cost you and how much you're willing to pay to reach the average TV viewer. What I'm talking about is not ratings or a show's share of the market, but the plain number of households you're paying to reach.

A simple tool known as the "Arbitron" book is an invaluable asset. All programming is broken into 15 minute segments. Each segment has a viewer rating that will tell you when the highest viewer draw is occurring. This will almost always, without fail, occur *within* programming, *not* during station breaks on the hour and half hour.

So, let's say you want to reach a wide audience. You'll find in the Arbitron book that a show has 100,000 viewers on the hour, 170,000 at quarter past the hour, and 125,000 viewers at the half hour. The show's a half hour long and you want to reach the most viewers. So, let's say you can pay $1 per thousand. Right away with the Arbitron book, you know that "best time" (say, 5:15 p.m.) is going to cost you $175. You know when you go into this whole thing just what you might expect and just what you can afford. Use such "beforehand knowledge" for yourself as background before you go into any of this. This way you won't walk out on a limb or find yourself half way out with no way to turn back.

HERE'S AN IDEA THAT COULD MEAN...

MONEY IN YOUR POCKET

Chapter Eight

Hot Tips For Big Bucks.

If you know how and why P.I. advertising works, *I* know you can make TV advertising turn out to be profit making beyond your dreams. I've given you not only the inside tips and step by step facts you'll need to do it, but I've also told you about the traps you need to look out for. Don't think just because there are some mistakes out there that I've told you about them to discourage you. Some old time advertisers might not even tell you what to watch out for. I just want you to know so you'll recognize the pitfalls and not fall in. Here are five more tips to keep the scales turned in your direction:

Tip #1—In the print media, (Magazines & Newspapers) a sales resistance exists at $29.95 for most products and, for written products (books and manuals) the figure might be said to be $12.95. Some say it's just today's economy, others say that's just a generalized rule of thumb. Anyway, high volume sales and the products designed specifically for that market have about a $30 limit. This is NOT true of the TV market. It's almost as if for the effort of reading your ad and cutting out a coupon, all you can get out of an ad reader is $12 to $30 dollars. But the TV viewer? He sits at ease while watching your ad—and then there's the lure and romance of the TV medium. That's why $395.00 and $199.00 are common place. Just one more reason why the TV medium is made just for you.

Tip #2—This applies to all media, written or electronic. Whenever you sell your product by the direct response method, have another product or book in the wings. Have literature you can send, another product you can offer while you have that customer's attention. After all, you paid good money to get his attention, so use it.

Tip #3—Depending on the product, depending on the market, depending on the show, or the season, whatever: small market stations can sometimes out-pull a major independent station in a larger city. I've had Po-dunk TV stations constantly outsell the larger cities sometimes. This just goes to say that you shouldn't sell the small market short. Don't assume you have to stick to the big cities or the popular shows. Nose around and use your instincts. Certain products will dry in the wind of one market and bring down the house in another. You'd be surprised how many times the "safe" rules can be broken, so be flexible.

Tip #4—Concerning C.O.D. orders: when you're getting a high volume response from your television ad, you can maximize on your profits by having a C.O.D. arrangement for orders coming in on an 800 number. There will be a rejection factor, though. Some people will actually refuse the shipment when the mailman brings the order, just to avoid the C.O.D. charge and nullify the order. You can cover your bet, if you want, by having all C.O.D. customers place a deposit to cover the costs of your handling and postage. (Personaly, I don't like C.O.D.)

Tip #5—Always send your tapes of an ad to advertisers by priority mail. I tell you this for a number of reasons. Whether you're sending dubs (a copy of your commercial) to a TV station or slicks (ready to run) of your ad to a newspaper or magazine, priority mail is double insurance. First of all, you get a receipt from the point of delivery. This "return receipt requested" step on your part protects you for several reasons. Primarily, if someone at a station tells you they haven't received your commercial, you've got someone's signature from the station in your hands. You can tell them who signed for it and, I'm sure, within minutes the station can locate your commercial that had simply been misplaced. This priority shipping acts as insurance. You're given a air-bill number from the post office or federal express against which you can have all your potential inquiries checked. After all your work, all your cookies are riding on this commercial. Just don't make a slip at the last minute and not pay any attention to how you send it out to the media.

OK, so now you see that I can show you how to make scads of money. You now know how to get the biggest advertising discounts when using glamorous television advertising. You even now know how to have that air-time for free whenever you want with a P.I. advertising program. It's now time for you to learn the most exciting angle you can ever use: writing, directing, and producing your own television commercial.

Listen, if I hadn't already let the air out of the whole world of television advertising, you might be amazed that I can put you behind making your own commercial. I've already told you the secrets and given you the knowledge you need for television advertising. It only stands to reason that I'd give you the biggest ace you'll ever need for guaranteed success. And I'll admit what no one else ever will: it's easy.

Now's the time to Take your best shot!

Chapter Nine

How To Make A TV Commercial.

There's no mystery to creating and making a television commercial. I've found it's not only easier than you think, but costs can be bone-thin. And profits fat. Believe me, the facts speak for themselves and I'm about to show them to you. Producing and directing a TV commercial has no more mystery than any new experience. Fascinating? Yes! Glamorous? Yes! Mysterious? No way!

Now, to make sure you deal the cards in your favor, I'll set up two rules I'll use to guide you. First, I want your commercial to stand with the best. To do that, I'll tell you, step by step, every ingredient you need, every move in the book that professionals use. Secondly, I'll not only tell you what you can expect in the way of costs, but I'll also tell you how each and every one of them can be cut dramatically. That's right, all the red tape, all the extra charges, can be avoided. I'll take that "gee, I don't know anything about it and besides it's probably too expensive" attitude and throw it right out the window.

Even a general knowledge of how to produce a TV commercial will lift the veil of mystery around television advertising. I completely understand how the average person might feel about television. It's there in our homes every day and statistics say the average viewer watches seven hours a day. You'd think that with something as familiar as that, we'd all understand it inside out. But forty years have gone by with TV in our lives. It continues to take us anywhere in the universe, forward or backward in time. It offers a thousand sights and sounds we might never have imagined. We're still in awe of that power. We attach a big mystery to how it wields that power.

Which is exactly why you know I'm telling you the truth when I say again and again that television is the advertiser's dream. Listen, if you've ever so much as worked with a printer to have a business card made up, you know there's no big deal to that. Maybe you "produced" something as simple as a wedding invitation, a birth announcement, or sent out party plans. What I'm teaching you here will be no more mysterious than that, believe me.

Now, I already know some of your first questions because I've been there. You want to know what you can sell and how you'll ever line up everything needed to begin filming your commercial. And, of course, you're waiting for the other shoe to drop concerning the subject of costs. Let me answer that first question about the product: it's a non-issue. What you sell with your commercial merely has to follow a very basic rule: it's not what you sell, but HOW YOU SELL IT! I'll show you cost and price ratios that are basic to TV advertising, formulas that insure maximum profits. But, as I said, that issue is on the side. What counts in any money-making effort is how you sell it. TV advertising takes care of that. Television is the most perfect "how to" that's ever come along.

It's the :60 (one minute) commercial for record albums, chore-saving gardening or workshop tools, convenience kitchen utensils or coin sorters, and decorative home items. This type of ad is always direct and simple, usually a demonstration style or audio sampling (with record and tape offers), and ends effectively with easy to understand ordering instructions.

You actually already know what you need to know to get in on TV's advantages.

But, like all new experiences, you think you don't know the first step and, if you let that stop you, you'll never proceed. Even if you did pick up on others' instructions, you then probably think you can't afford it. Well, the "I don't know how to do it and besides it's too expensive" attitude might have you closing the door, locking it, and throwing away the key before you even start. But once you've got a $6 or $8 cost item that you could sell for around $20 or $30, wouldn't you want hundreds of thousands of orders while spending only a couple of hundred to make a commercial and spending no money at all for advertising time? Well, it can be done, you're going to learn how and you're going to do it.

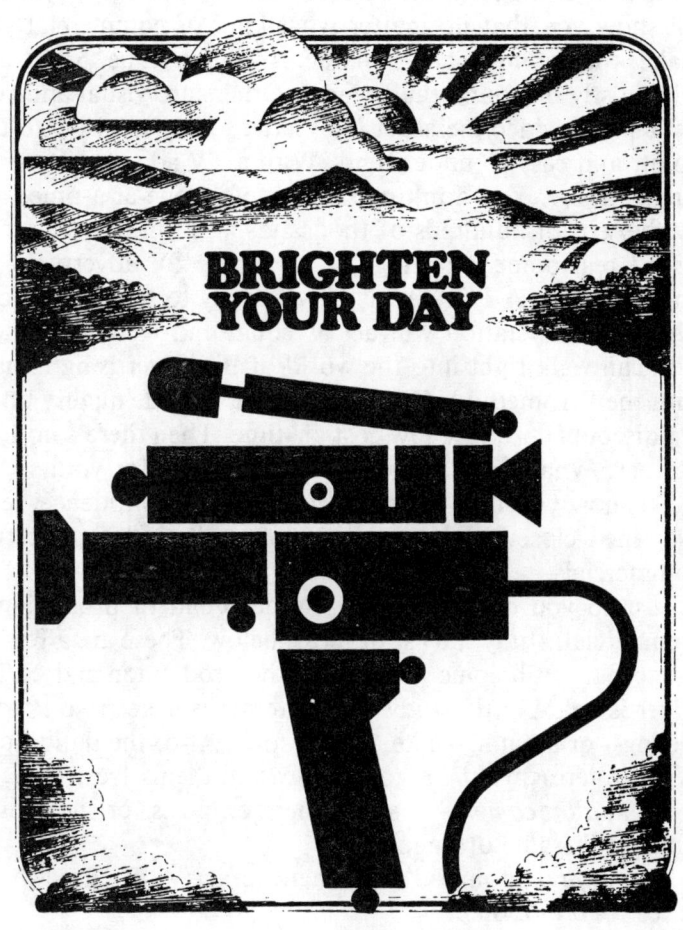

Let's divide the entire task between two things you need to do: produce the commercial and get it on the air. Boiled down so "simply" as that, you wouldn't know where to start. But it's a simple matter once you know how. You don't have to take my word for it. The facts I'm giving you demonstrate the simplicity. The facts will state the case for me.

As far as producing the commercial is concerned, you need three things: the idea, the visual direction, and the execution. I'll show you that no matter what kind of commercial you make, the commercial's "character" is the same. Some ads rely mostly on sound (audio ads). Others are visual and rely on a strong video message. No matter. They're brief, to the point, and easy to understand. With a TV ad, your buyer is already there. You don't make your offer one-at-a-time, but by the tens of hundreds of thousands at a time.

The real point is having the power of TV advertising at your disposal. A P.I. deal is good money to the TV station. That's why a station will act as equal and willing partner. You can walk right into the world of Big advertising money with the P.I. method. Or, when you buy a little quality time, big discounts produce low cost air-time. Then there's no P.I. partner. What then? Just even bigger money for you!

To show you how to start with ease and confidence, let's examine—close up—the makings of audio and video script commercials.

Just so you can jump into the deep end of producing a commercial, study the list of terms below. These are a few of the terms you'll come to know in the production end of TV advertising. A little study of the terms will keep you from feeling—or seeming—like a greenhorn. Also, the definitions of these terms will be a good education themselves.

Animation camera—a still camera on posts for shooting a single still frame of animation

Animator—an artist/draftsman; draws stills used in a series for "motion"

ASCAP—American Societey of Composers, Authors, and Publishers; the organization that controls and supervises paymens of royalties and fees

Close Up—a close photo of product or actor; also called CU; ECU = extreme close-up; MCU = medium close-up

Composite track—the final mix of the soundtrack

Cut—a break of filming when action is complete; term also used in editing: a straight cut = a scene change without disolve or fade

Demo—a demonstration tape or sample of a musician or announcer

Disolve—the overlapping fade in/fade out of scenes (long or short)

Fade—as in "fade-in" or "fade-out"; also "UP" or "DOWN"—from black to scene or scene to black

IPS—Inches Per Second"—term for sound tape (3 and 3/4, 7 and 1/2, or 15 IPS); a speed measurement: the faster the IPS, the higher the sound quality

In Sync—action matched with sound

Leader—the attached threading lead-in, numbered 10 through 2 (there is no 1 or zero)

Lip Sync—actor filmed with lip movement; also "M.O.S.—"without sound" (no lip movement)

Optical window—a small segment of a frame with a scene used at the commercial's end; shows address, product logo, and ordering instructions.

Ones, twos, threes—a term from animation: still drawings that change each frame, every other frame, or every three frames. Resulting effect is smoothest (ones), smooth (two)s, or jumpy (threes)

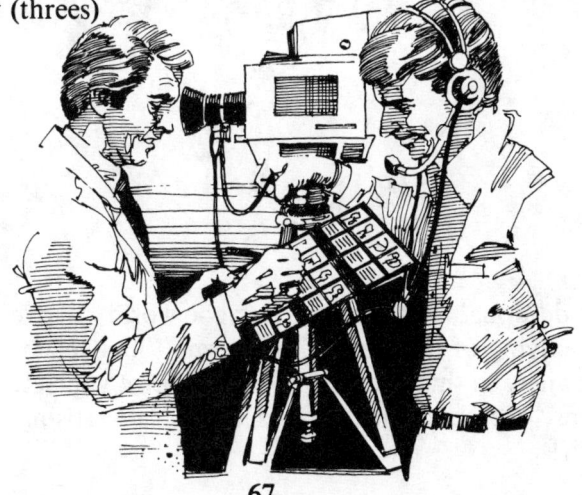

Rotoscoping—mixing animation with live action scenes

Stock footage—previously shot scenes of all kinds filed in film libraries. A charge for making a print of stock footage might be paid PLUS a fee for actual footage used. Usually live, some animation

Take—each time you shoot a scene is a take; "take one, take two" etc.

Voice-over—VO—announcer's voice (or actor) on the soundtrack; not in lip sync with action

Additional terms are found in the world of advertising and the buying of air-time. Those terms I'll cover in "live use" elsewhere in this book. If you familiarize yourself with these terms, the thrill and success of TV advertising will teach itself!

Chapter Ten

How To Make A Sound Track in A Recording Studio.

Naturally, the kind of product you want to strive for is one that has a proven track record of high volume sales. You're using television, so look at what has done well with that method of advertising. You might as well accelerate your success by going with a product tailor made for TV.

Record albums. *Any* record album. You've seen seasonal music, comic music, rock and roll, religious, *any* kind of record album is tailor made for television. Records are a different kind of product than gadgets, tools, or items for personal use. You can demonstrate the *use* of a kitchen tool. A stand-up presenter can show a TV viewer the fun of a toy. But a record album? It doesn't *do* something, it isn't operated. But an album has *sound*. Sound sells a record album. And, because half of TV magic is sound, what you have to provide is an attractive soundtrack. You must also provide the other half of TV magic: sight.

Sight of a record album can be a sleepy matter if all you did was put the album cover up on the screen and did nothing further. That's why, when you see this type of ad, there's a "roll" of song titles moving across the screen. So, the sight angle in this type of ad is a listening demonstration, not a visual demonstration of use. There's no personality standing there talking, explaining how to use something. Instead, there is the visual image of the album, the visual "rolling" of song titles. The camera may move while filming the album, but actually all this "movement" are images of *un*-moving still pictures.

While I'm on the subject of the "sight" angle of "sound" selling, let me point out that there's more to a record than the album cover. Often there are lyric sheets. You're going to cover all the bases when selling a record album. In doing that, there will be 8-track tapes and cassette recordings to offer along with the LP. In the fashion of a display ad, all these items can be laid out on the screen. It helps the viewer understand the worth of your offer when he sees all that can be bought.

You can also expand the "feeling" of your music with other still pictures. If you had an album of classic music, you could use quiet pastoral scenes or pictures of historical moments. If you were selling religious music, you could show pictures with religious settings along side your album. Rock and roll? Get pictures of hamburger stands, old cars, young people on the beach. You get the picture. Whatever visual scenes your music identifies with can provide "movement" to your record album advertising.

But sound is really what this type of selling offer is all about. You've got to give the customer a "taste" of what he or she can have, you've got to let the viewer experience the product. This will be your main objective. Just don't forget that while you emphasize the sound of your product, the accompanying sight angle shouldn't be boring. Both the sight and the sound portions of your commercial should heighten each other. One angle shouldn't water down the impact of the other.

If you had a product that sold by having a stand-up presenter demonstrate its use, that would be your sight angle. But sound is what sells a record album. So in the case of record album sales, you need to have a sound track recorded for your commercial. You need to be selective in that you put into that soundtrack. The music will sell to whatever segment of the public likes that particular sound. For that reason, the music you "show"—by way of sound—should grab the viewer's attention.

You'll be picking selected bits of certain songs on that album that "demonstrate" to the customer that this or that album has what they like. If it's religious music you're selling, give the TV viewer peaceful, inspirational, or classic hymns to hear. On the other hand, if it's rock and roll that's offered, make sure the beat is prominent, the pace hot. The pieces of music you select could have the titles prominent in the lyrics.

Such an arrangement could coincide with the visual rolling of titles. You've got to strike the music lover where he lives. It might be the beat, the tune, the group or performer. What I'm saying is study your music. Music has the same USP as any other product—its Unique Selling Position. Use it.

I would urge you to immerse yourself in the album you select to sell. Play it nearly night and day until you're steeped in the sound of what the album offers. I want you to come to know that album inside out. Now you're ready for the first step in creating the soundtrack for your commercial. I want you to select the ten best songs from that album and get out a tape recorder, any tape recorder will do. Decide for yourself, out of each of the ten songs, what 20 second segments best identifies that song. It may be lyrics, it may be instrumental, the song will govern that angle. It could be a chorus line, a familiar musical passage, you get the idea. Play around with the 20 second segments you single out of each of the ten best songs on the album. When you've got these recorded, you've got the raw materials for your soundtrack. Right before your eyes (or ears, actually), you'll begin seeing the finished product unfold.

Now you have 10×20 seconds, or 200 seconds. This soundtrack portion of the commercial is going to be a large part of a :60 commercial, so here comes your second step: select out of each 20 second segment a short segment, 6 to 8 second long, that really captures, really zeros in on that song. When approaching this step in the sound track production, all that listening and absorbing of the album really pays off. When you have put together the ten songs and whittled each one down to 6 to 8 seconds, the finished product has become the main body for your commercial. There was time involved in arriving at this point, but not too much sweat. So far, so good.

So, you say, when does the hard part of this commercial making begin? I got some "bad" news for you: it's over and done with. The main body of your commercial has been produced. Now you have 10 song selections, each 6 to 8 seconds long, and twice the material needed to produce the :60 album commercial. Five of these selections will wind up being used in the ad. The other five will act as the necessary back-up in the world of soundtrack recording. Anything can happen in the recording studio where the soundtrack will be professionally prepared. The studio boys know their business inside out. Their ears are in touch with what sounds best flow into another sound. Trust me—and trust them. You'll be armed with plenty of ammunition for them to work their magic when they put approximately 35 seconds of music together for you.

So now you're ready for the out-of-the-house portion of making your soundtrack: the recording studio. Don't jump back or faint, this is the fun part! It's no more difficult than anything you've done so far. Even someone who isn't selling a record album will sometimes find that music belongs in his commercial. It's at this point that both the item seller and the album seller can be helped by the outside professionals.

But I'm still not talking about agencies or studios with sky-high fees for time and expertise. Sure, you could go out and pay big money for studio time. Is that all you have to do with your budget? I told you back in the beginning that I'd not only tell you exactly how to get great quality into your commercial, I'd also tell you how to pare the costs to the bone. There's no exception here. Red tape was meant to be cut. Read on.

Let me lay out for you what you've got so far. Here's how all the elements of your commercial will be laid out to make up the audio/sound portion of the ad:

1. You or someone else introduces the product, the album. The first thing heard on the soundtrack is this announcer telling the viewer: "Here's Vic Damone's favorite collection of classic songs! They'll take your heart around the world and your memories back in time. Travel along with these favorites."
2. Right after this brief introduction will come the music portion of your soundtrack. You've already got that: the five segments, 6 to 8 seconds each, making up about 35 seconds of this soundtrack. (Bear in mind, what's happening here is the audio portion of mind, what's happening here is the audio portion of the ad. The visual portion of the advertising—song titles rolling by, lyrics, visual scenes, etc.,—all come later when you're in the filming stage of production.)

3. Following right after this music portion of the audio track comes what's know as the "tag." All commercials in direct response advertising have a tag. This is a 15-18 second "space" for final selling of the product. This portion of the audio track is where the pricing and ordering information is presented. Also, and this is as important as putting water in the pot when you want to make coffee, the tag is a two-part time space. On the first part of the tag you put, as I said, the price and ordering instructions. Sample: "Here's how to order: Send $8.95 for albums or $9.95 for 8-track or cassette tapes to Vic Damone—" "You'll quickly see that this doesn't take 15-18 seconds, but right after "Vic Damone—" comes a blank space. Each television station that handles your commercial will then insert specific ordering directions and their mailing address—such as: "Station KDTT-TV, Box 98, Pittsburgh, Pa." So, you see, that 15-18 second tag will contain both your announcer's "set up" for the ordering instructions *and* the broadcasting station's own announcer giving the mailing address information. Here's how it runs together:

Your Announcer: "Here's how to order: Send $8.95 for albums or $9.95 for 8-track tape or cassette to Vic Damone..."

TV station announcer: "Station KDTT-TV, Box 98, Pittsburgh, Pa. That's $8.95 for albums or $9.95 for 8-track tape or cassette to Vic Damone, KDTT-TV, Box 98, Pittsburgh, Pa."

So there it is, a package for a :60 commercial. You've got somewhere just short of ten seconds for offer introduction, about 35 seconds of an audio track, and at least 15 seconds for ordering information. Keep this structure in mind. You're about to proceed to the sound studio.

Don't worry about finding a sound studio. There are more of them all over the place than you might imagine. Some are practically in your own backyard. You'll have to make sure they have the right equipment for the job, but that's no problem either. What you're interested in is getting the job done right and done at the right price. Here's my suggestion:

Get out the trusty phone book and scan the listings of the radio stations in your neighborhood. Maybe you have some large network affiliates in your town, but I'm going to suggest that you give your attention to the smaller stations. Give them a call and simply state that you are interested in having them record the audio portion of a soundtrack that is going to be used for a television commercial. Simple, straight facts, right? Believe me, they're used to this. They'll either tell you they can do the job or they haven't got the equipment to do the job. Well, you can go on to the next station if they can't handle it, but most stations not only have the equipment, they also have a studio for the recording, too. And what do you think they're doing with all that equipment and the studio while they're on the air with music? Producing soundtracks, naturally. So go right ahead and just lay it out. But not all of it. Pricing comes next.

Next they're going to want to ask how long you need and maybe they'll go right into quoting you a price by the hour. That can start as low as 25 bucks and go right on up through the ceiling. Here's the tip: always try to downplay the time factor. If you walk right into paying by the hour, somebody somewhere is going to wind up taking their time and driving your studio costs higher than heaven. Tell them it's not going to run anywhere near an hour, and maybe it might not run a half hour. Tell them you're running very little announcer scripting and mostly splicing 30 seconds of music selections. If they're even a little hungry for your business, a job rate, not an hourly rates may be offered.

Here's your next tip: they're already thinking when they can next work you into their schedule. Tell them time isn't pressing you and offer the following deal. Tell them you want to use their facilities on "down-time" and offer a flat $50. They'll either take it or not, real simple. Understand this: "Down-time" is time that they're not using the equipment themselves, plus they haven't got anything else, or any one else, scheduled to use it. Down-time happens and if they let it go by, that's money they didn't make and the opportunity won't come again. This doesn't mean you'll be showing up in the middle of the night. Technicians aren't there anyway. It's simply empty time and you're offering them money for it.

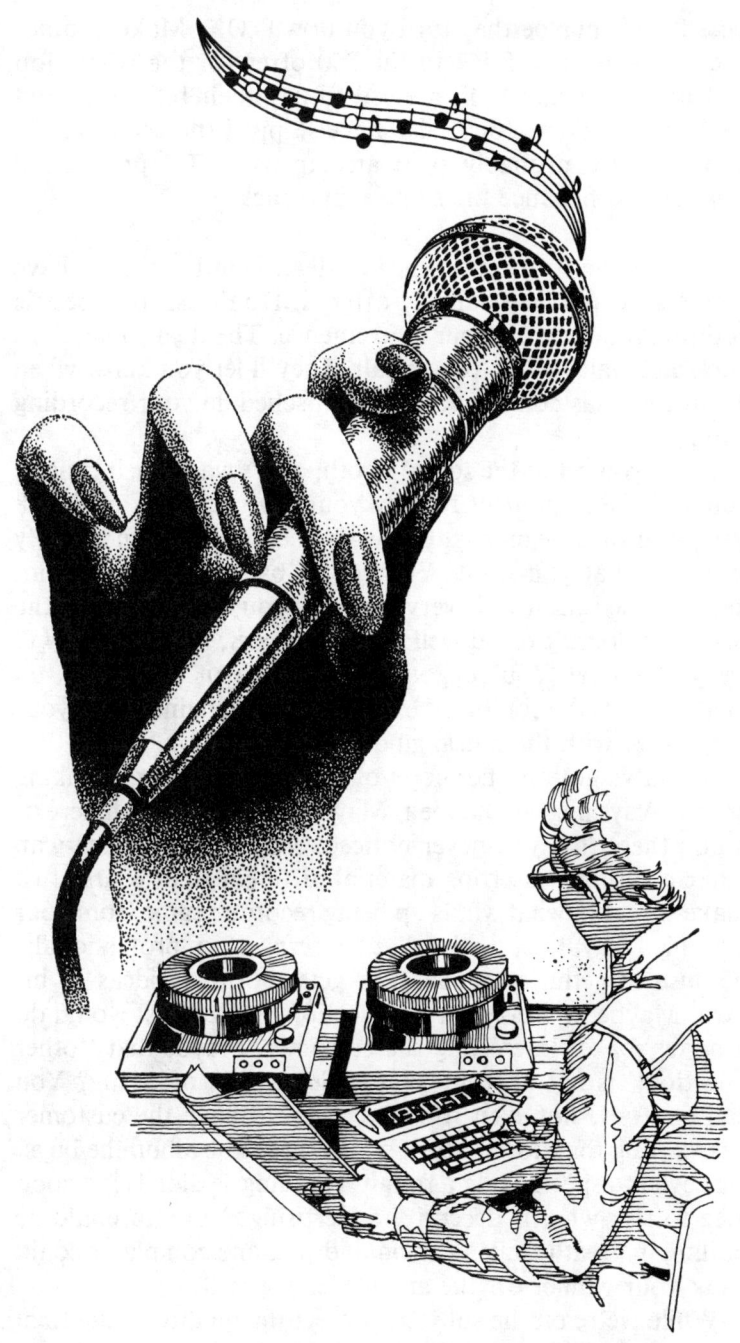

Like I said, maybe they turn you down. OK. Make another two or three calls. Stick to the $50 offer for the whole job (not at hourly rates). They need to pay their bills, too, and you'll get a taker. You'll also have skipped the $400 to $500 someone else probably paid an expensive TV production company to produce the same soundtrack.

OK, you've struck a down-time deal. Don't expect to have a date and time immediately offered. Don't ask for specific additional favors for your convenience. The deal's made. Sit back and wait for the phone call. They'll let you know when down-time has come up and they'll schedule your recording date.

When you get to the sound booth, don't waste their time or yours. Take a moment to play your ten selections of 6 to 8 second musical segments for the engineer. Plainly and simply tell him what you want. You've got back-up material with half your selection and everything else you need. If one of the segments doesn't blend well into the others, the engineer will let you know. You've got substitutes with your back-up material. Let the combined expertise of the engineer and your familiarity with the music guide you.

If you've got another copy of the album, you're thinking ahead. Anything can happen. Maybe there's a scratch here or a pop there that you never noticed. Maybe the engineer can make a case for inserting material different than yours. Just make sure that what winds up being recorded came from your album. I say this, with all due respect to professionals, because sometimes the engineer gets too many ideas of his own. Maybe he feels another selection by the artist would do a better job of interesting the customer. Maybe that "other selection" is not on your album. See what I'm saying? You can't afford, not even for 6 seconds, to have the customer hear a song that doesn't turn out to be on the album he buys. Not even to speed along a rough recording session is it a good idea to risk what is deceptive advertising. Your ad could be pulling in great results later on and just one complaint could yank your winner off the air. Cover yourself.

While we're on the subject, protect the quality of the final soundtrack. Don't settle for quality lower than your highest standards. You're not out to appear unprofessional in your total ad effort. Don't skimp here on the audio portion. If you're not satisfied with the product in the studio, don't walk out or miss the simple opportunity to have it done again. You're paying for the job and the job's not right until it's right. Every little part of your commercial that's second-rate will have a very adverse effect on your total product. So, if something doesn't sound right, get it corrected right away while you're in the studio.

Careful, though. Don't hop up and down in the sound-booth. Don't be a pain to deal with. Don't insult the abilities of the pro's you're working with. You're entrusting them with your sweetheart, so don't cross the fine line between wanting perfection and getting the whole deal called off. If you don't handle this just right, they're not going to offer another down-time deal to you ever gain. Listen, no matter how exacting I have been with sound people, camera people, or studio technicians, I never met anyone in the business who didn't know what they were doing. They wouldn't be there in the first place if that wasn't the case. They love their work and they're good at it. They'll give you more than 100% effort, that'll show. Easy does it (but cover yourself!). Good relations will always pay off many times over in the long run.

OK, somebody else's work is now behind you. Here's what you have: a soundtrack for the audio portion of your commercial will be on a reel-to-reel tape—NOT a cartridge or cassette. You SHOULD get cassette recordings as copies from the studio. These easier to use cassettes will give you an at-home tool in further shaping the rest of your commercial. You'll be using this audio portion to plan and build around when it comes to constructing the visual portion of the ad.

By the time you leave the studio with your recording, prepare an AUDIO SCRIPT and a time-table for the soundtrack. When it comes time to direct the visual portion of your commercial, this audio script will give you a framework for the next step. Here's what an audio script might look like:

AUDIO SCRIPT

1. 8 sec. ANNOUNCER: (Intro.) "Here's Vic Damone's favorite collection of classic songs! They'll take your heart around the world and your memories back in time. Travel along with these favorites!
2. 8 sec. MUSIC: "I left my heart in San Francisco..."
3. 7 sec. MUSIC: "The first time I saw Paris..."
4. 6 sec. MUSIC: "Baloons over Cherbourg..."
5. 7 sec. MUSIC: "Blue Moon of Kentucky..."
6. 6 sec. MUSIC: "My China doll..."
7. 6 sec. ANNOUNCER: (Tag) "Here's how to order: Send $8.95 for albums or $9.95 for 8-track tape or cassette to Vic Damone—"
8. 12 sec. These remaining 12 seconds of the tape are blank and will be used by each of the TV stations that broadcast your commercial. They will include a mailing address, sometimes repeating the pricing information, and may repeat the whole tag a second time if space permits.

TOTAL TIME: 60 SECONDS.

Chapter Eleven

How To Make The Visual Half of Your Commerical.

Now you've got the audio portion taken care of. Your next concern will be the visual half of the commercial. In another section of this I'll insert product sales, but for now let's carry the album sales idea forward. With the audio script, written and counting, you should set up a visual script right along side of it.

Let's say, along with the album cover, possible lyric sheets, the 8-track and cassette tapes, you also wanted to use some still pictures. Visual scenes parading past the eye, can give "movement"" to the commercial. In the case of the Vic Damone album I've been using as an example, pictures from around the world might be pleasing to the eye. If I was using a country music album, scenes from mountains, forests, farms, or pick-up trucks might be just right. I'd probably pick out at least eight, maybe ten, pictures that suited my album. These will provide "motion" and visual content to the ad. Once I've done this, the process of putting together a commercial is just about done.

Out of my ten pictures, each plays an important role. I'll select one for my introduction, either a large panoramic view or one involving people close up. Next, I'll refer to my audio script and line up an appropriate picture for each of the songs in the soundtrack. In a bit I'll tell you about video terms, but here, with my pictures, I may want to blend a couple of pictures to go with one song. As the songs change, a fade-out of one picture and a fade-in of another will make for smooth visual changes. Just starting and stopping pictures and songs could come off too abruptly. I want a seamless, professional look to my finished product.

The last picture the viewer will see isn't a picture at all. It's a shot of the product. The album cover, the LP, the 8-track and cassette tapes will be spread out on the screen. Now that

I've laid out these visual ingredients, I'm ready to add the video portion of my commercial to the audio script that's already been constructed. Let me show you how to arrange this blend of video and audio scripting:

:60
Vic Damone Classics

VIDEO TIMING
CUES FOR PICTURES

VIDEO		AUDIO
1. 8 sec. Opening Shot, The Picture of San Francisco Bay Bridge, dissolve to next shot	-0 sec.-	ANNOUNCER: (intro) "Here's Vic Damone's favorite collection of classic songs! They'll take your heart around the world and your memories back in time! Travel along with these favorites!
2. 8 sec. man and woman walking hand-in-hand near cable car in S.F., dissolve to next shot	-8 sec.-	MUSIC: "I left my heart in San Francisco..."
3. 7 sec. Paris streets, Eiffel Tower, cut to next shot	-16 sec.-	MUSIC: "The first time I saw Paris..."
4. 6 sec. balloons rising in the sky, dissolve to next shot	-23 sec.-	MUSIC: "Baloons over Cherbourg..."
5. 6 sec. country picture, Appalacia, dissolve to product shot	-29 sec.-	MUSIC: "Blue moon over Kentucky..."
6. 7 sec. product shot, cut to tag	-35 sec.-	MUSIC: "My China doll..."
7. 18 sec. Tag superslide black and white to be colored electronically blue background, gold letters	-42 sec.-	ANNOUNCER: (tag) Here's how to order: Send $8.95 for albums or $9.95 for 8-track tape or cassette to Vic Damone—!!

8.   -48 sec.-   The remaining 12 sec. of audio is blank and is to be used by each individual station announcer to insert mailing address. Complete tag is repeated if time permits.

9. Special video instructions: Crawl begins 8 seconds in from the start of commercial using the bridge photo as a cue. Ends 34½ seconds in, just prior to the product shot.

As you can see, the video portion actually lays out the order of visual scenes that match up with the audio portion. Your entire script is just about done. The only thing left to do is schedule a taping date and get this on film. Allow me to explain a few undefined terms in the script that I'm using for an example. Also, let's cover each "second of importance" in the commercial.

1. The picture of the San Francisco Bay Bridge comes on the screen just as the announcer begins introducing the album. At 8 seconds into the commercial, the bridge picture fades into the two lovers and cable car picture.
2. At the 8 second mark, the song, "I left my heart..." begins as the second picture of the two lovers appears. This segment takes another 8 seconds. Then the picture fades out, the next picture fades in.
3. At the 16 second mark, 16 seconds into the commercial, the second song begins with the third picture, the picture of Paris. The second song in the audio portion begins. This is a 7 second segment. The picture of Paris fades out and we fade into the next picture.
4. We are now 23 seconds into the commercial. The next picture fades in as the next song comes up. After this 6 second segment, we cut to the next picture. Before we have used slower, smoother fade-ins and fade-outs. A "cut" is a quicker visual change.

5. Here we have the Appalacian picture and a 6 second segment of music. Fade to product shot.
6. The commercial is now 35 seconds from start. The visual image now is the product shot, the audio portion is on another song. This segment is 7 seconds long and here the tag begins. While the product is being shown, prices appear with the record itself, the 8-track tape, and the cassette. While this segment quickly cuts to the tag, the station which films the commercial will take care of the price appearing on the screen. This is done electronically in the following manner.

   The pictures which mix with your audio track have been filmed on easels. At least a couple of easels will be used. Two or more cameras will film the picture on the easels fading back and forth as pictures are changed on easels not being filmed. Or, they may set three pictures on three easels, film each with succeeding three cameras, stop, and change the three pictures. Then they'll shoot again the same way, producing six of the pictures. Each station will have their own way of doing this.

   Now when it comes time for the product shot, on another easel you'll have your product(s) laid out, taped to a 4' × 4' posterboard. Use an ordinary tape, but be certain to secure the items well and not let any of the tape show. A process sometimes called superimposing will be typed on a screen called character generating. This is done with what is essentially a computerized electronic typewriter.
7. At 42 seconds into the commercial, the tag appears on the screen. This initial tag comes from a 35mm black and white slide. Have this slide made for you by the station before you come for the filming. The cost will be no more than $6 and will look like this:

$8.95 Albums   8-Track and Cassette $9.95

VIC DAMONE

As you can see, this is only a partial tag because the rest of it will be filled in by individual stations airing the ad. For this reason, when you have this partial tag prepared, tell them most particularly that it should cover only the upper one-third of the slide. First because it will be easier for the viewer to see that information on the screen and, second, because you want to leave room on the screen for the mailing informating that's added on later. Be sure to get this part right.

You might notice I stated two certain colors to be electronically used on the black and white slide. I designated one light color, gold, and one dark color, blue. There are still quite a few black and white TV's out there in use today, some are small portables scattered around the house, right? Well, if two light colors were used or two dark colors, they just wouldn't show up on a TV set that sees only light and only dark.

When that tag appears on the screen, it's going to be there for 18 seconds (42 seconds have gone by). But, and don't overlook this fact whatever you do, only *6* seconds of audio will be there for that 18 second space. Only a partial tag is happening in those 6 seconds.

8. After the 6 second partial tag has passed, 48 seconds of the :60 commercial have passed. The video portion is still running, the product shot. In the remaining 12 seconds, the individual TV stations will insert the address for mailing. They may even repeat the ordering instructions from the beginning if they have time.
9. Notice those "special video instructions" at the end of the script? Wondering what a "crawl" is? Simple. On the same computerized electronic typewriter the titles of various songs on the album will be prepared. This "crawl" begins (check those instructions) 8 seconds after the start of the commercial and ends about 34½ seconds worth of song titles being "rolled" or "crawling" across the screen.

As you might be able to plainly see now, a lot of motion, or apparent motion, has been added to an otherwise motionless commercial. It has no people. It has no action. But it has visual content: changing pictures, crawling titles, fade-ins and fade-outs, quick cuts—in fact, 'round the world travel!

Chapter Twelve

How To Make A Product Commercial

So, now we've covered one type of scripting for TV advertising. But maybe you're not going the album route, maybe you'll be using a product and it needs demonstration, salesmanship. I used an album as an example to show you how to script without personalities, letting the product do its own work. And besides, as you might well imagine, albums do extremely well being advertised on TV.

The next time you're viewing television commercials, stop and notice the :60, 1:30 or 2:00 commercial. To put on the next hat of producer, study the commercials you've seen often. Again, notice what ingredients are in those commercials: display, demonstration, use explanation and ordering instructions. Practice "selling" your product to yourself, cutting out the unnecessary phrases and factors that don't add to pitching that product. Pattern your speech to those ads you see on TV.

Write your advertising copy as you would speak to someone you know, use the informal, neighborly nature of your ad's medium. Try it on the phone with a relative or neighbor, there's nothing to get uptight about. Tape the sound portion of one of those TV ads. Write it out as it's delivered and pattern along side it your sales talk. Once written, record yourself giving your sales talk and compare it to the one taped from TV.

Bear in mind that when you come to your finished product you will want anywhere from 12-20 seconds at the end for the repetition of your product's name, it's price and further ordering instructions. So you actually have approximately forty seconds in a :60 commercial to do your actual product introduction, demonstration, and selling. Now you know why some of those old-fashion :30 or split-:30 (15 seconds) commercials weren't around very long. No one could convincingly sell anything in so short a span of time or the rush of words necessary to attempt effective salesmenship. Fortunately, TV stations have returned to the full :60, :90, and 2:00 commercial formating. Television may serve us with entertainment, but the business they're in is the selling of time, commercial time. The longer commercial lengths are simply easier for them to fill if they don't have to chase down a half dozen advertisers to do it.

When preparing a script of your commercial, organize both the written equivalent of the selling speech along side your concept of what video images will occur step by step. Using a blank page, arrange the audio portion of the script down the right hand half. Down the left hand half of the page, write out a visual description of what will be occurring at each point in the speech. Type this up neatly and in large print so there'll be no mistaking things later on. Having rehearsed your selling numerous times long before actually filming of your commercial may make the script seem needless later, but the filming studio is going to need to actually see what is expected.

By now you see that you are the famous talent that's going to star in your commercial. You've already skipped an ad agency's fees by creating your own script. Besides, who knows better than you just what your product is and how it works. Now you've again skipped the high costs of TV advertising by not paying a professional announcer to read your script. The time that an announcer would need to familiarize himself with your product and learn his lines will turn out to be time saved and money not spent.

So how do you get your prepared product and script on film? Even if you need further demonstration of script format, call a local television station. That's where 90% of all local ads are filmed. Tell them you'd like to speak to an engineer and tell the engineer that you'll be having a commercial filmed at his station soon. Ask him when they'll be filming a commercial which you could sit in on to see how they handle things. Promise the engineer you'll be quiet as a mouse and stay out of the way.

This step in your endeavor is important. It's going to give you experience in the atmosphere of commercial filming and

HERE'S SOMETHING TO THINK ABOUT

Be a Part of the Action

prepare you for your own day in front of the camera. You'll become accustomed to the movements of the camera and sound personnel, the language, the lights and sets. Watch for whatever ease or ineptness someone else displays in doing their commercial. Without getting in the way, observe how the technicians work with a script, learn what's easy to understand and what gives them problems. These are all things that you want to avoid when your day comes. You can pay several visits to the station or others. This is free time and worth countless dollars in experience.

By stepping through each production factor apart from the actual filming, you'll gain the necessary professionalism your commercial deserves. Not a penny has been spent yet in getting your ad on the air. Don't wait until you're paying for production and filming time to know what you want and how it will be done. By pre-production day, you'll have the station, script, and filming sequence prepared and lined up on paper. In working with yourslef this way, don't accept an "I'll work that out later" attitude as a response to problem areas.

You may find it useful to write several different script approaches, even if you ultimately come back to your original version. While the "stand-up presenter" format will be the leanest and most direct approach, other formats are also widely used by commercial producers. Obviously, "personality testimonial" would be costly, as would animation. With animation there would be the costs of a cartoonist or illustrator, as well as the slow frame-by-frame filming if more than still shots were used. Music can be employed along with a spoken script without excessive costs. This approach would involve recording an audio tape at a facility separate from the TV station filming. The costs would be additional to filming, but need not be excessive due to the availability of "down time" at a local radio station. Just as in preparation for TV station filming, you should be thoroughly prepared with musical excerpts and timing requirements before spending money with the recording studio.

Theatrical approaches are always available to advertisers. While these involve greater depth in scripting, TV viewers may find them more entertaining. Two formats using nonpersonality actors would be "real people" responses and opinions to the advertised product or a "slice of life." In this format, a "problem" situation is set up which is resolved by the purchase of the product. Clogged drains and soiled shirt collars have for years demonstrated that a product can restore harmony to life and relationships. Such situational script formating can be appealing, but bear in mind that other persons' costs arise and the difficulties of sets and acting can lengthen film time and, thus, re-shooting costs.

The least expensive format of self-presentation is by no means less effective than all other script types. The presenter can be female or male, can appear friendly or authoritative, and can use props (other than product) or costumes. Translating your knowledge and faith in the product to someone else can result in a fumbled or watered down presentation, so self-presentation is highly recommended not only for cost-saving reasons, but for time and believability factors, too. The demonstration, use, or comparison action of your product in use convinces TV viewers that the product is simple to use and gives the buyer a sense of what the product does and how it works. The commercial should also convey to the buyer that it will work as well for them and accomplish its function. Your ad concept should highlight the "USP"—the unique selling proposition" of the product. The USP pushes the product's inherent function and desirability.

Don't be afraid to use maximum verbalization or illustration. After all, your using television, the medium of sight and sound. Visualize your customer and design your commercial to make him or her receptive to your product. Keep as a yardstick factors which may seem so obvious to you, but are things you must not, for that reason, overlook. Is your ad simple and direct? What is the intent of your commercial and does it do what you originally wanted it to do? Don't get lost in the tiny details to the point that you lose your way among the trees. The apparent large forest of television advertising is indeed full of many paths. What is important to you is that you not meander about with unnecessary path-finding, but that you go straight through as easily and as inexpensively as is possible.

Which brings us to the cost factor of filming your commercial. If you had been told at the beginning that you were going to spend as little as $200 in getting your ad on the air, you might not have found it believable. So you see that filming costs are your primary financial concern. But because you will be using down-time at a TV station to have your commercial produced, you're avoiding cast and location costs and ad agency fees and a hundred other expenses that would forever keep TV advertising beyond your reach.

Professional filming and editing of your commercial is the most necessary ingredient in your total effort. As in standard mail order business, the best product at the best price can't get anywhere with poor packaging, unprofessional sales literature, or sloppy order forms, return envelopes and the like. As said before, about 90% of all local station advertising is filmed at the station. The engineers and sound crews do this every day and make their living at it. Private film houses may have flair, an artful approach, and be fun to deal with, but they also command handsome fees for their time, equipment, and ideas. Business is business and the no-nonsense approach of low cost TV station filming has more going for it than just low overhead.

Pricing your filming will require a few phone calls. It would be advisable to begin with your local stations (non-network) or the local stations of nearby cities. Talk to the engineers, not sales people, at first. The engineers or production people can tell you what's impractical, costly, or they might be able to suggest other alternative film approaches. At this point you're looking for ball park figures only, not exact prices. A tight budget for a large advertiser might be $50,000. A local company might consider $1,000 to be their most minimum investment. Think of filming in a smaller city, not New York, Los Angeles, Chicago, etc. You'll want to request 16 mm, not 35 mm or video production. Using a small city local station and a half hour of set time, costs of $500 or less are easily attained. With a little patience, waiting till the station is experiencing slow business, they'll be willing to give you the time your commercial requires for filming for about $200. Obviously, you've presented yourself as a competent person, but along the way you didn't appear to be spending honest truth of wanting to get this ad on film for as little cost as humanly possible is a good approach to use when committing yourself to the film crew. It's not new to them and they can appreciate your situation. They've done it before and you'll generally be a very capable hands.

Basic points not to be forgotten are getting a price quote on filming that includes final editing and more than one copy of your commercial. "Buy *by* the job," not "by the hour" whereever possible. Shopping around is always a good idea in any case, even if you have to travel a few miles to get the job done for the price you want. You may be quoted a "firm" price which includes the film company's costs and their projected profits. The other price quote might be "cost plus/fixed fee." This price structure involves the cost of production exclusive of profit and a stated fee which is fixed based on time and other factors which is their profit. Your research of phone calls or visits to the station will give you what you need to make your decision.

Let your film people know that you'll be doing direct response advertising. This means that you want to have a blank 12-15 second "tag" at the end of your ad. It is on this "tag" (usually with a silent background of your product and its price) that a later announcer will give ordering instructions by the station that airs your commercial. This is why your script and filming time will run :45 for a :60 commercial. You may have decided to go with a :90 or 2:00 ad for greater showing of your product, but if you are presenting the selling and demonstration of your product in the :60 format, :45 is what you have to work with.

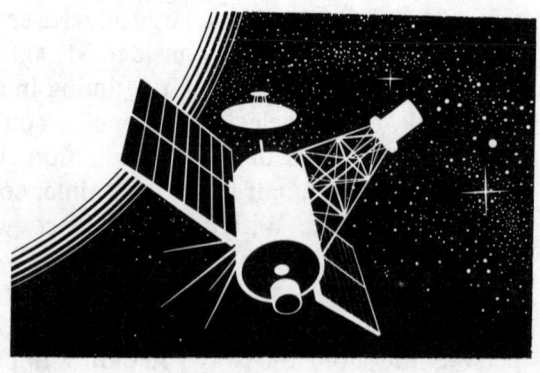

Chapter Thirteen

Three Tips for TV Station Filming

Whether you market mostly an audio, video, or a combination style commercial, a few additional instructions should be given to the TV station filming crew. When you arrive for the filming, your script is basically what everyone will follow. It's a fairly simple document. It was laid out simply so you could construct the commercial. It's simple so that the crew won't have any problem understanding what actually needs to happen. But, because there are always minor differences, one station to the next:
—Always bear in mind the essence of what you're doing here: you are selling the product. You want to do this well, but entertaining an audience is not a main concern. In all direct response advertising, what matters is that you sell the product. Don't get too caught up in that old romance over the idea of television. Frankly, and let me speak plainly here, a lot of special effects could be conjured up by station engineers. But what good is it if your viewer is dazzled by the ad so much that he forgets what's being offered? We've all seen wondrous ads that entertain us no end—and we love to see them again and again—but who remembers what it was all about? "Wow!" you say, "but what were they saying?" It happens. Even the glossiest commercials and the biggest budgets get sold a bill of goods that way. Don't blow it by trying to blow the audience away, that's all I'm saying.
—Don't forget the element of motion. Whether you're demonstrating a product in use or show basically still pictures to sell your product, motion can be essential. Simply have a camera angle change or create a zoom effect with a camera moving in on the action. An old rule of thumb is that on TV, where audience-attention span can be dreadfully short, 4 seconds is about the limit for no motion at all. For example, an 8 second shot can be broken up with a fade-in, a zoom in

or out or a different viewing angle than the last picture, and a fade-out. Just don't let your picture, what the viewer sees on the screen, just sit there. The viewer won't wait for you.

—ALWAYS ask if the station has a character generator. Almost all stations do, but some may not. Others may have their's "down" at the moment. So don't assume anything. Ask! Having a character generator create the "crawl" effect is the best way to go. But don't panic. If the engineers tell you they have no character generator, they may tell you they can produce the same effect in other ways. There are other ways, true, and they can be almost as good, in fact OK. But having a character generator to do this is best. It produces the most professional finished look for your commercial.

Ready To Go

So now the station filming is done. It's an incredible feeling, I know. But don't run out of the station right away. Have the technicians run the ad for you, just for the fun of it. Watch it a good two or three times. You'll find it fun and fulfilling. After the fun's out of the way, now have them run it and pay good, I mean real good, attention to it. Be critical. Maybe the few times through, you were so overwhelmed and satisfied that you missed a shot or two that's out of focus. Maybe the crawl is fuzzy or slow. Too fast maybe? Are there any little white spots on the film from time to time? A jiggle here or there you want to get rid of? Now's the time to do it. You've paid maybe $250 or less for the job and now's not the time to run out before the job's done really well.

So now you have a copy. It's called a master and it's the only one in the world. I very strongly urge you to have a second copy made. It's called a second generation submaster. This submaster should be made immediately. All additional copies will be "dubs" of this second generation submaster. You master becomes a permanent copy, unused for any further work on the commercial. Never let this master out of your possession. Never use this original copy of your work to be sent to a station instead of a dub. Never send this copy out to have copies made. It might never happen, but once, just once, a copying facility or a station will damage, lose, or somehow ruin this finished work if you send it out. Store it at home in a cool, dry place. It should only be used to make additional submasters for when you need to have further copies made.

Chapter Fourteen

Untapped Hong Kong Manufactures.

If you're looking for great products for your TV Campaign. The following is a list of overseas manufactures that are anxious to sell their products here in America. Drop them a line, and tell them what you are looking for, they will be more that glad to send you wholesale price lists, catalogs, and free samples.

Grand Dragon Universal Sales Co. Ltd.
Lee Chau Commercial Building
5/F., 11 Hart Avenue
Tsimshatsui
Kowloon, Hong Kong
Ultrasonic pest repeller, electronic rat repeller DC 9 volt, or AC adaptor 110V or 200V, electronic & ultrasonic items.

Honour Electro Works Ltd.
Tsing Yi Industrial Centre, Phase 1, T.Y.I.
Lot No. 65, Blk. B4, 6/F.
Tsing Yi, N.T., Hong Kong
Battery-operated tinplate or emergency signal flashlights, M300 with magnetic.

High Technology Manufacturing Ltd.
6/F., Flat D, I & J, Fu Cheung Centre
No. 5-7 Wong Chuk Yeung Street
Fo Tan
Shatin, N.T., Hong Kong
Large size ultra-violet insect bug killers, lure range from ¼ to 2 acres with 15-40 watt ultra-violet tubes & 1500-4000 volts/9mA on metal grids.

Chi Lick Electrical Manufactory Ltd.
2/F., Unit B, Kwai Shing Industrial Building
36-40 Tai Lin Pak Road
Kwai Chung, N.T., Kowloon
Electric fuses for radio & TV, automobiles, household & industrial uses & fuse holders.

Kay Kwong Electric Bulb Fty. Ltd.
27-29 Tonkin Street
Wai Tak Industrial Building, 7/F.
Kowloon, Hong Kong
Zenon flash tubes, neon lamps, neon tubes with reflector, electronic flashing lights operated with zenon flash tube, component: trigger coil, sub-miniature toy's bulbs, krypton bulbs.

Man Shing Electrical Manufactory, Ltd.
Flat B, 2/F., Kwai Fong Industrial Building
9-15 Kwai Cheong Road
Kwai Chung, N.T., Hong Kong
Bakelite products.

Man Boon Manufactory Ltd.
Flat A, B, 8/F. & Flat B, 7/F.
Cheung Yick Industrial Building
12 on Yip Street
Chaiwan, Hong Kong
Coaxial cable CATV, 5ATV, 5C2V, 3C2V, RG types, speaker cable, audio screened cable, 9.5mm RF plug/socket lead, audio DC plug lead.

Metro & Co.
Flat D-I, 13/F., Blk. B
Marvel Industrial Building
17 Kwai Fung Crescent
Kwai Chung, N.T., Hong Kong
Adjustable lamps, ceiling & wall lamps, crystal chandeliers & electric water heaters.

Nam Wah Electrical Factory
Unit 1, Blk. A, Hang Wai Industrial Centre
T.M.T.L. 114, Kin Wing Street, N.T.
Hong Kong
All types of bakelite electrical accessories of international specifications & standards.

Polly Houseware Limited
Room 801, Wah Kwong Regent Centre
88 Queen's Road, Central
Hong Kong
Decorative, industrial, desk rotary fans, batteries (9V, R20, R14 & R6), extension reel cord & all other electrical appliances.

Samson Products Factory
Tuen Mun Industrial Centre
13/F., Flat E-4, TMTL 76, Pui To Road
Tuen Mun, N.T., Hong Kong
Plastic products.

Tai Kwong Electric Mfg. Co. Ltd.
928-930 Cheung Sha Wan Road, 3/F.
Kowloon, Hong Kong
Bakelite & rubber electrical accessories.

Wing Tat Shing Mfg. Co. Ltd.
10/F., Flat A, Manning Industrial Building
118 How Ming Street, Kwun Tong
Kowloon, Hong Kong
Electric cable, PVC power cord sets for electronic appliances, communications cable & low-voltage wires for automobiles.

Value Pool Manufacturing Co. Ltd.
Blk. C4, C9, C10, C14, 16/F.
Belya Industrial Centre, Shek Pai Tau Road
TMTL 164
Tuen Mun, N.T., Hong Kong
Heavy duty rubber flashlights & other rubber products.

Yao Sheng Enterprises Ltd.
111-113 Lai Chi Kok Road, 1/F.
Kowloon, Hong Kong
Bulbs, sole distributor of "Polar Bear."

Dickie Plastic Fty. Ltd.
Flat C, 11/F., Shui Wing Industrial Building
12-22 Tai Yuen Street
Kwai Chung, N.T., Hong Kong
Candy novelties & candy containers for all seasons.

Yuk Sung Industrial Corporation
9/F., Lyton Building
46 Mody Road, Tsimshatsui
Kowloon, Hong Kong
Auto-lit cigarette case combined with cigarette case lighter & ash-tray in plastic cabinet.

Everwin Industrial Mfy.
Blk. D, 22/F.
Melbourne Industrial Building
16 Westland Road
Quarry Bay, Hong Kong
Metal & plastic giftware, souvenirs, advertising premiums.

Floral Trends Ltd.
Unit 501 Houston Centre, 63 Mody Road
Tsimshatsui East
Kowloon, Hong Kong
Florals, foliage & Christmas decor.

Genuine Associates (Sundries) Ltd.
51 Man Yue Street, Kaiser Estate (Phase 2)
Top Floor, Flat L
Kowloon, Hong Kong
All kinds of home decorations & wooden housewares, wooden/metal framed pictures & pub-mirrors, glass decorative plaques, plastic/aluminum photo frames.

Hong Kong Candles Manufactory
Blk. 19, 16/F.
Wah Luen Industrial Building
15-21 Wong Chuk Yeung Street
Fo Tan
Shatin, N.T., Hong Kong
Birthday, relight, party candles.

Highlands Silver Plate Co. Ltd.
Room 913, Nan Fung Centre
TWTL 258, Castle Peak Road
Tsuen Wan, N.T., Hong Kong
Silverplated, goldplated & brassplate giftware & tableware, custom made projects such as trophies, pitchers & commemorative plate in the silverplate & goldplate, inscriptions of name, logo & scenes can be done on most items.

Hoda Company
G.P.O. Box 10153
Hong Kong
Oil & traditional Chinese paintings with a variety of subjects. Portraits from individual photos & copies of old masters.

Hong Fuk Co.
Blk. E, 12/F., Sui Sham Industrial Building
8-10 Kwai Shau Road
Kwai Chung, N.T., Hong Kong
All kinds of mobiles, hanging, tale, ball tree, car & plastic miniatures in different models.

Islandcan LImited
13/F., Granville House, 41C
Granville Road, Tsimshatsui
Kowloon, Hong Kong
Decorative tinware. Canister sets, trays & coasters, promotional items.

Inter-Pacific Supplies Co. Ltd.
G.P.O. Box No. 2664
Hong Kong
Collection of tinsel garlands & Christmas decorations.

Johnny Supplies Ltd.
Flat A3, 14/F., Hankow Centre
47, Peking Road, Tsimshatsui
Kowloon, Hong Kong
Artificial green foliages, flowering plants, flower bouquets & bushes, feathered birds & items, cake decorations, party favours & year round festival novelties.

Chapter Fifteen

Untapped American Importers.

If you're looking for quick products for your TV Campaign, and you don't want to deal with companies out of the U.S. Then the following is a list of American Importers that are anxious to sell their products to new mail-order TV houses. Drop them a line, and tell them what you are looking for, they will be more that happy to send you wholesale price lists, and catalogs.

A Classic Time Watch Co.
1225 Broadway, Suite 811
New York, NY 10001
Watches, melody alarms, desk & travel clocks.

A & A Electronics Co.
435 Los Angeles Street
Los Angeles, CA 90013
Electronics Products, clocks, calculators, watches.

A-B Emblem
Division of Conrad Industries
P.O. Box 695
Weavervile, NC 28787
Swiss embroidered emblems, promotional caps & jackets.

AHM-Regal Way Inc.
P.O. Box 235
El Toro, CA 92630
Electric trains, accessories in H.O. scale and N scale, battery operated flying airplanes.

A K International
40 North Water Street
Lititz, PA 17543
Photo frames in solid brass, silver plate, wood, plastic, stone, shell and more.

AMF Alcort
520 West 15th Street
Oshkosh, WI 54901
Sailboats & sailboards.

AMF American
200 American Avenue
Jefferson, IA 50129
Exercising machines.

Accurate Leather & Novelty Co. Inc.
1731 West Belmont Avenue
Chicago, IL 60657
Ladies' and men's leather goods, purses, wallets, etc.

Accutime Watch Corp.
1239 Broadway
New York, NY 10001
Full line quartz watch starting at $3. Designed with own logo.

ACOR Plasticover Co. Inc.
50 Cooper Square
New York, NY 10003
Custom printed tote, sports and garment bags.

Action Fashions Inc.
3339 W. Diversey Avenue
Chicago, IL 60647
Fashion design, liquid-insert Tee shirts & other wearing apparel.

Action Recliners by Lane
Highway 45 South, P.O. Box 1627
Tupelo, MS 38802
Rocker recliners or Wall Saver recliners.

Active Generation
2924 Main Street
Dallas, TX 75226
Jackets, caps, embroidered emblems.

The ADCAP Line
1400 Goldmine Road
Monroe, NC 28110
Promotional painters caps and aprons, tote bags, baseball style caps, bicycle caps & bandanas.

Kurt S. Adler Inc.
1107 Broadway
New York, NY 10010
Christmas decorations includes ornaments, table giftware, trees, wreaths, train sets, etc. Special projects welcomed.

Advance International Inc.
1200 Zerega Avenue
Bronx, NY 10462
Craftkits, Lil Missy doll kits, Christmas ornament kits.

Advance Watch Co. Ltd.
26400 West 8 Mile Road
Southfield, MI 48034
Quartz LCD and analog desk clocks & watches, novelty timepieces, alarm clocks.

Airline Textile Manufacturing Co.
2145 West Jackson
Des Moines, IA 50315
Bags of all styles including duffles, garment, totes, golf, import, etc.

Airway Industries, Inc.
Airway Park
Ellwood City, PA 16117
Travel bags, business cases.

AKAI America Ltd.
800 West Artesia Boulevard
Compton, CA 90224
Hi-Fi audio systems, VHS video recorders, radio cassette portables, etc.

Alabaster Industries
Industrial Road
Alabaster, AL 35007
Complete line mugs, tumblers, pitchers, kitchen ensembles & refreshment sets.

Aladdin Industries Inc.
703 Murfreesboro Road
Nashville, TN 37210
Thermos bottles, lunch kits, picnic baskets & coolers, etc.

Alafoss of Iceland
c/o National Incentive Resources
151 First Street South
Winter Heaven, FL 33880
Icewool by Alafoss, Icelandic woolen apparel, accessories & blankets.

Alger Creations Inc.
50 South 4th Street
Brooklyn, NY 11211
Inflatables.

Algoma Net Company
1525 Mueller Street
Algoma, WI 54201
Sport bags, hammocks, benches, luggage.

Alladin Plastics Inc.
Phipps Bend Road
Surgoinsville, TN 37873
Imprinted plastic housewares & premium sets.

Allied Plastics Inc.
1663 Hargrove Avenue, P.O. Box 974
Gastonia, NC 28052
Automobile accessories including travel mugs, holders & snack trays, tool totes, whisk brooms, oil drain pans, funnels, & oil spouts.

Allied Premium Company
1170 Broadway
New York, NY 10001
Daher Ltd. metalware trays, etc. from England. Toys by Amtoy & metal recipe files by Syndicate Mfg. Co.

Aloha Candle Co. Tapa Design Hawaii
P.O. Box AC
Kaneohe, HI 96744
Aloha wear, souvenirs, Hawaiian table line and beverae napkin.

Alpha Products Inc.
2110-C Northwest
Marietta, GA 30067
Ultravisor, inflatable pillow & cushion.

Alsip & Company
2310 Upper Farms Road
Bainbridge Island, WA 98110
Executive hardwood games from New Zealand, Australia, US. Handmade gift items by Cottage Industry in Pacific Northwest.

Alvimar Mfg. Co. Inc.
51-02 21st Street
Long Island City, NY 11101
Plastic inflatables, for premiums, point-of-purchse displays, etc.

Ambur Electronics Inc.
1344 South Commerce Road
Walled Lake, MI 48088
Telephone Accessories.

AMCA International
2701 Industrial Drive
Bowling Green, KY 42101
Chain saws, paint sprayers, electric soil blender power digger, etc.

AMCAM International Inc.
308 Wainwright Drive
Northbrook, IL 60062
Prinz photo, video, consumer electronic items.

Block's
23720 Crosson Drive
Woodland Hills, CA 91367
Live exotic plants for mail order, guaranteed drop ship service, packaged display assorments.

Blondy Art Luggage Inc.
2375 Ekers Avenue
Montreal, Quebec, Canada H3S1 C6
Custom made sports bags, fiberglass insulated coolers, garment bags, cosmetic & toiletries bags, automobile front covers.

Bone Promocionais Torino Ltda.
Rua Joao Teodoro 1614
Sao Paulo, SP Brazil 03009
Bonnets, promotional bonnets in cotton & cotton/polyester.

Book Sales Inc.
110 Enterprise Avenue
Secaucus, NJ 07094
Books.

Bose Corporation
2345 Millpark Drive
Maryland Heights, MO 63043
Direct/reflecting sound systems

Botica Commercial Farmaceutica Ltda.
Avenue Rui Barbosa, 3450
Sao Jose dos Pinhais, PR Brazil 83100
Cosmetics, toiletries, shampoos, soaps, children's bubble bath.

Boxes by Pandora
125 Main Street, Box 284
Springfield, MA 01101
New custom made wood boxes in walnut, cherry, oak, redwood, etc. Solid brass boxes & painted boxes feature combination locks. Inhouse engraving & silk screening.

Jonathan Bradley Pens Inc.
50-02 Fifth Street
Long Island City, NY 11101
Writing instruments, desk accessories, custom & private label work.

Branco International Inc.
234 Fifth Avenue
New York, NY 10001
Tube Clock by Mueller & Van Dongen, a unique promotional item. Quality Irish crystal & marble desk accessory line.

AMEREC Corporation
1776 136th Place, NE
Bellevue, WA 98005
Exercise equipment including Tunturi bicycles, rowing machines, jogging machines. Pulse meters and vital signs monitors.

American Accessories Inc.
(Fran Stef/Epco)
10 West 33rd Street
New York, NY 10001
Nylon & synthetic custom manufacturing of wallets, purse accessories, travel bags, etc.

American Cyanamid Company
One Cyanamid Place
Wayne NJ 07470
Lightsticks.

American Engravers Inc.
CM Corp.
6689-L Peachtree Industrial Boulevard
Norcross, GA 30092
Etching of quality crystal glassware to your specifications, both single & double depth etches.

American Heritage Industries
3400 West Grand Avenue
Waukegan, IL 60085
Deep engraved personalized glassware, stemware, etc. Featuring monograms, family crest, custom logos, etc.

American Household Products
1709 Dunnavant Road
Leeds, AL 35094
Small plastic houseware items, includes mugs, insulated ware, nite lights, etc.

American Idea Marketing Corporation
100 Main Street
Reading, MA 01867
Market introduction to a variety of new products geared to premium trade.

American Intercontinental Trade Group Inc.
21250 Califa Street, Suite 109
Woodland Hills, CA 01367
Solid brass executive accessories, coasters, paperweights, desk & wall clocks, etc.

American Jewelers Inc.
71 Fifth Avenue
New York, NY 10003
Manufacturers of gold watches, diamond jewelry & rope chains.

American Premium Corp.
125 Walnut Street
Watertown, MA 02172
Jigsaw puzzles, presto magix transfers, iron-ons, calendars, corrugated items, inflatables, adult premiums, self-liquidators, etc.

American Products Group
11 John Street, Suite 806
New York, NY 10038
Imprintable Mylar sunglasses.

American Sports International Inc.
P.O. Box 527 Midway Station
Tallahassee, FL 32343
Fitness equipment, exercise bicycles, rowing machines, aerobic weights.

American Thermometer Co. Inc.
P.O. Box 1509, 125 Bacon Street
Dayton, OH 45402
Microencapsulated liquid crystal temperature sensing devices and other thermometers.

American Tourister Inc.
91 Main Street
Warren, RI 02885
American Touister luggage for men & women. Cases, garment bags, sets.

American Umbrella.
45 West 18th Street
New York, NY 10011
Umbrellas, bags, garden/beach umbrellas, rainwear.

Americana Art China Co. Inc.
356 East Maryland Avenue
Sebring, OH 44627
Mugs, ashtrays, plates, decorated glass with custom logos.

Amity Lamp Corporation
441 High Street, Box 367
Perth Amboy, NJ 08861
Lighted advertising displays & sales incentives, complete line lamps & lampshades.

Amity Leather Goods Co.
735 South Main Street
West Bend, WI 53095
Men's & women's personal leather goods & related products.

Amster Novelty Co. Inc.
75-13 71st Avenue
Middle Village, NY 11379
Cosmetic, jewelry & tote bags, soft sided luggage, scented items & novelties.

ANACAPA Corp.
25933 Frampton Avenue
Harbor City, CA 90710
Plastic colored handled flatware, kitchen tools, patio lamps, children's backpack & lunchbox.

Anagram International Inc.
5575 West 78th Street
Minneapolis, MN 55435
Metallic balloons.

Anchor Hocking Corp.
109 North Broad Street
Lancaster, OH 43132
Glass tableware & ceramic dinnerware, glass & plastic conventional & microwave ovenware.

ANDIS Company
1718 Layard Avenue
Racine, WI 53404
Personal care appliances, hair dryers, curling brushes & irons, hair cutting kits.

ANGLAF Corporation
428 Kings Highway
Brooklyn, NY 11223
Imprinted Scrimshaw, bar accessories, games, wall decor, miniature ships in bottle, etc.

Anglo Affiliated Company
1133 Broadway
New York, NY 10010
Plastic inflatables designed in unusual & creative shapes for marketing or merchandising need.

Animal Fair Inc.
7780 Brush Lake Road
Minneapolis, MN 55435
Stuffed animals, puppets, costumes, etc.

ANSCO Photo-Optical Products Corp.
1801 Touhy Avenue
Elk Grove Village, IL 60007
Disc, 110 & 35mm cameras.

Apatche Badge & Emblem
111 West 40th Street
New York, NY 10018
Woven patches, emblems & appliques, wooden bookmarks, lables & trim. Cloisonne pins.

Apple Computer Inc.
20525 Mariani Avenue, M/S 23-EB
Cupertino, CA 95014
Apple Personal Computers.

Apple Premium Products
184-08 Jamaica Avenue
Hollis, NY 11423
Inkless fingerprint system for children, home security alarms, household adhesives, etc.

Aquascooter Inc.
79 Hazel Street
Glen Cove, NY 11542
The maneuverable, submersible 2-hp engine that can pull you through the water at more than 4 miles per hour.

Argold Internationale Ltd.
63 Daniel Street, P.O. Box 731
Farmingdale, NY 11735
Fireplace furnishings, giftware, decorative accessories.

ARITA
2345 Millpark Drive
Maryland Heights, MO 63043
Fine dinnerware.

Arnart Imports Inc.
212 Fifth Avenue
New York, NY 10010
Norman Rockwell Figurine Americana, Art sculptures, boutique mugs, etc.

Arrow Trading Co. Inc.
1115 Broadway
New York, NY 10010
Full line of Pierre Cardin quartz clocks, novelty phones, calculators, stationery.

Art-Mold Products
(Pierre Cardin)
30 Kennedy Drive
Cranston, RI 02920
Pierre Cardin elegant gift ensemble of diaries, desk accessories, distinctive gifts, etc.

Bridgeport metal goods Mfg. Co.
365 Cherry Street
Bridgeport, CT 06605
Flashlights, lanterns, portable lamps.

Brigade Brands Ltd.
2345 Millpark Drive
Maryland Heights, MO 63043
Gucci watches.

R.A. Briggs & Company
650 North Church Street
Lake Zurich, IL 60047-0468
Beach & bath towels, bath ensembles, custom embroidered toweling, aprons, golf, novelty & tennis towels & ponchos.

Bright Products Inc.
P.O. Box 14000
Roanoke, VA 24022
Hot plaques, coasters, memo boards, picture magnets, recipe cards, etc.

The Brinkmann Corp.
4215 McEwen Road
Dallas, TX 75234
Thermos, lanterns & stoves, spotlights, grills.

Brinson Corp.
887L Industrial Road
San Carlos, CA 94070
Portable thermoelectric refrigerator/warmers.

British Royal Mint
Kaller & Associates Inc.
275 Liberty Avenue
Westbury, NY 11590
British Royal mint, gold, silver & base metal presentation coinage of the UK.

Broadway Photo Inc.
777 Bloomfield Avenue
West Caldwell, NJ 07006
Personalized photo items.

Brockway Standard Inc.
16 Daniel Road
Fairfield, NJ 07006
Stronghold utility box.

Brooklyn Products Inc.
9201 Wamplers Lake Road
Brooklyn, MI 49230
Custom printed foam products, balls, car care products, toys & other premium items.

Brookpark Plastics Inc.
Expo Mart—Suite 268W, 105 Mall Boulevard
Monroeville, PA 15146
Melamine dinnerware, servingware, children's sets, household items.

Brother International Corp.
8 Corporate Place
Piscataway, NJ 08854
Electronic typewriters (computer compatible), personal electronic printers, portable sewing & knitting machines.

Buccaneer Mfg. Co. Inc.
35 York Street
Brooklyn, NY 11201
Athletic, recreational & leisure wear.

Buck
520 West 15th Street
Oshkosh, WI 54901
Knives.

Bulova Watch Company Inc.
75-20 Astoria Boulevard
Jackson Heights, NY 11370
Watches & clocks.

Burlington Basket Company
P.O. Box 808
Burlington, IA 52601
Hampers, wall shelves, wastebaskets, tissue boxes, sewing chests, space savers, tables.

Burnes of Boston
200 Wells Avenue
Newton Center, MA 02159
Photo frames, promotional frames, novelty frames.

Burwood Industries
4655 West Chase
Chicago, IL 60646
Clocks, decoratie wall accessories, home furnishing.

Business Marketing
220 East 42nd Street
New York, NY 10017
Various issues of our magazine & other promotional materials.

Butane Products Corp./
Baldwin American Mfg. Co.
820 Merrick Road
Baldwin, NY 11510
Pocket & table cigarette lighters, smokers' articles, gifts, writing instruments, etc.

Bear Archery
4600 S.W. 41st Boulevard
Gainesville, FL 32601
Complete line of archery equipment, back packs, camping tools & lanterns for outdoor & hunting.

Beck Shoe Polisher
Division Sutton Ind. Inc.
21 Cherokee Drive
St. Peters, MO 63376
Electric shoe polishers, shoe care items, custom shoe shine kits & shoe bags.

Bee Plastics Corporation
511 Lancaster Street
Leominster, MA 01453
Ice chests, cooler chests, personal coolers, dispenser jugs & picnic jugs.

Beemak Plastics
7424 Santa Monica Boulevard
Los Angeles, CA 90046
Plastic literature holders & dispays for brochures, forms books & any type advertising materials.

Belcrest Inc.
320 West Commercial Avenue
Moonachie, NJ 07074
Decorated glassware, china, plastic, metal & wood, by decal, banding, screen printing, etc.

Belding Sports
1504 South Flower
Los Angeles, CA 90015
Golf bags & accessories.

Cosco Inc.
2525 State Street
Columbus, IN 47201
Step stools, counter stools, cars, folding tables & chairs, gas & electric mono-filliment trimmers & edgers, juvenile products, etc.

Costa Electronic Inc. USA
2023 West Carroll Avenue, Suite 200
Chicago, IL 60612
Quartz wall clocks, business card holders, timers, night lights, etc.

Cottonluxe Mfg. Co Inc.
71 Mall Drive
Commack, NY 11725
Tote bags, drawstring bags, aprons, log carriers, T-shirts, zippered cases.

Counselor Company CM Corp.
6689-L Peachtree Industrial Boulevard
Norcross, GA 30092
Bathroom scales, mechanical, fiber optic electronic, digital, custom sales.

The George F. Cram Co. Inc.
P.O. Box 426, 301 South LaSalle Street
Indianapolis, IN 46206
New Concept globe models, maps & calendars.

Basketville Inc.
RD No. 1
Putney, VT 05346
Handwoven hardwood baskets & solid Northern Pine
buckets, pine collection & occasional furniture.

The W.E. Bassett Company
259 Roosevelt Drive
Derby, CT 06418
Nail clippers, tweezers, emery boards, nail files & other
manicure implements.

Bausch & Lomb & Bushnell
Div. of Bausch & Lomb
1400 N. Goodman Street
Rochester, NY 14692
Ray Ban sunglasses, magnifiers, binoculars, telescopes, rifle
scopes, sport glasses.

Bavaria Ltd. Inc.
P.O. Box 36
Reamstown, PA 17567
Authentic German steins, steins & beermugs for
customizing, crystal steins & trophies.

Bay State Specialty Co.
2 Rice Street
Middleboro, MA 02346
Creative plastic housewares, ice scrapers, key tags, note
holders, magnets, magnifiers, etc.

Beacon Enterprises
937 Saw Mill River Road
Yonkers, NY 10710
Health & exercise equipment.

Beacon Products Corp.
9 Lincoln Street
Newton Highlands, MA 02161
Volari deluxe plastic stackables, mugs, ice buckets, pitchers,
basic housewares, etc.

Beaird-Poulan/Weed Eater
5020 Flournoy Lucas Road
Shreveport, LA 71139
Gasoline chain saws, electric & gasoline line trimmers.

J&J Beall Woodworking
541 Swan's Road, N.E.
Newark, OH 43055
Original design wall & shelf clocks from American
hardwoods. One-of-a-kind wood sculptures.

Crosby Concept
804 Stump Road
Chalfont, PA 18914
custom packets vegetable, flower, herbs & tree seed, oyster mushroom spawn, tropical air plants, bird houses & feeders.

A.T. Cross Company
One Albion Road
Lincoln, RI 02865
Cross writing instruments & desk sets.

Crown Craft Products Inc.
22 West 21st Street
New York, NY 10010
Premium & mail order items, men's gifts, pocket knoves, brassware, etc.

Crown Herald Inc.
6106 Benjamin Road
Tampa, FL 33614
Desk memo & pen sets, wall & desk clocks, tape measurers, flashlights, etc.

Crown Publisher Inc.
One Park Avenue
New York, NY 10016
Hardcover & paperback books, featuring travel related series. New line video cassettes.

Conrad Bell/USA
1441 Broadway
New York, NY 10018
Leather briefcases, portfolios, journals, travel bags, small personal.

Benay Albee Nov. Co.
52-01 Flushing Avenue
Maspeth, NY 11378
Novelties, toys, souvenirs & custom imprinted headwear.

Bennett Brothers Inc.
211 Island Road
Mahwah, NJ 07430
Hard-cover 518 page merchandise catalog, choose-your gift selective gift programs for bank promotions, etc.

Benrus/Clinton/Fantasy
1104 South Wabash Avenue
Chicago, IL 60605
Watches & jewelry of every description.

Crandall-Hicks/Puch
250 Eliot Street
Ashland, MA 01721
Puch Austro Daimler lighweight bicycles & Puch mopeds.

Cravat Club Inc.
443 Hicks Street, Suite 6H
Brooklyn Heights, NY 11201
Manufacturers & designers of quality corporate neckwear, club ties, scarves, bow-ties, etc.

Creations by Alan Stuart Inc.
398 Fifth Avenue
New York, NY 10018
Designer cosmetic brushes & accessories, shampoo & soap dispenser, small leathergoods, luggage, pens.

Creative Cookie Company Inc.
3900 16th Street NW, No. 388
Washington, DC 20011
Specialty fortune cookies, Jewish, Irish, Italian, Hispanic, birthdays.

Creative Designs Inc.
Premium Sales Division
P.O. Box 33101
Louisville, KY 40232
Purveyors of fine "marquetry," natural wood mosaic art formed into clocks & picture frames.

Creative Embroidery Corporation
211 Grove Street
Bloomfield, NJ 07003
A complete direct embroidery service including tape punching. Jackets in satin, wool, leather, etc.

Creative Glass Inc.
P.O. Box 269
Kalamazoo, MI 49005
Wood products.

June Critchfield Designs
1126 Greenridge Land
Pittsburgh, PA 15220
Canvas items including tote bags, aprons, book covers, pillows, pot holders, game seats, etc.

Criterion Watch Co. Inc.
60-01 31st Avenue
Woodside, NY 11377
Criterion Electronic quartz analog & digital watches & clocks.

Berg Products Design
P.O. Box 401
Lake Bluff, IL 60044
Fashion plastic server sets, party goods, storage items & totes.

Berkey Marketing Companies
25-20 Brooklyn-Queens Expressway West
Woodside, NY 11377
Camera & video tripods, bags, cases, flash units, camera lenses.

Berkley & Company Inc.
Trilene Drive
Spirit Lake, IA 51360
Fishing, tackle, outdoorsman gift items, water sports equipment.

The Berkley Publishing Group
51 Madison Avenue, 22nd Floor
New York, NY 10010
Publisher's of mass market & trade paperbacks.

Russ Berrie and Company Inc.
111 Bauer Drive
Oakland, NJ 07436
Plush animals, soft sculptures, porcelain dolls, mugs, stickers, card lines, novelties, etc.

Best Emblem & Insignia
636 Broadway
New York, NY 10012
Emblematic jewelry, embroidered patches, web belts with logo buckles, logo incentive programs.

Betra Plastics Inc.
P.O. Box 6325
Spartanburg, SC 29304
Platic drinkware, mugs, coolers, pitchers, visors.

BIC Corporation
Special Markets Division
P.O. Box 2001
Largo, FL 34294-9990
BIC writing instruments, lighters, shavers.

Bildan Corporation
1081 Bristol Road
Mountainside, NJ 07092
Sony, Fisher, Seiko, Toshiba, Panasonic, Sharp, Sylvania, GE, Philco, Akai, Admiral, Hamilton Beach, etc, diversified products.

Binney & Smith (Crayola) CM Corp.
6689-L Peachtree Industrial Boulevard
Norcross, GA 30092
Crayons, markers, art kits, advertising specialties, hobby crafts.

Bionaire Corporation
565 A Commerce Street
Franklin Lakes, NJ 07417
Air purifiers, humidifiers, floor care systems, outdoor cooking systems, computer accessories.

Birdie by Richard A. Leslie Company
578 Nepperhan Avenue
Yonkers, NY 10701
Outerwear of nylon, poplin, corduroy, wool melton, golf jackets, conditioning suits of coated nylon.

Bissell Inc.
2345 Walker Road, NW
Grand Rapids, MI 49504
Carpet sweepers, vacuum cleaners & shampooers, electric warming trays, housewares, buffet accessories.

Black & Decker Corp.
701 East Joppa Road
Towson, MD 21204
Bench & stationary tools, power tools and household products, lawn & garden tools.

Blaisdell & Co. Inc.
112 Park Street
North Attleboro, MA 02760
Promotional jewelry.

Brans Nut Company
581 Bonner Road
Wauconda, IL 60084
Gift packs of eating nuts, natural foods, popping corn, candies, maple syrup, wild rice.

Brazilian Government Trade Bureau
551 Fifth Avenue
New York, NY 10176
Advertising specialties, incentive & gift programs.

Dan Brechner & Co. Inc.
50 Carnation Avenue
Floral Park, NY 11001
Gifts

Briarcliffe Studio, Inc.
230 Philadelphia Pike
Wilmington, DE 19809
P.J.'s (Carousel Horse replicas), personalized professionals, gourmet foods.

Mackler Productions
Rt. 541, Box 328
Lumberton, NJ 08048
Complete line of children's & adults imprinted sportswear.

Mag Instrument Inc.
1635 South Sacramento Avenue
Ontario, CA 91761
Aluminum lifetime flashlights D.C. & AA size plus 30,000 candle power rechargeable system.

Magnaform Corporation
305 East 63rd Street
New York, NY 10021
Pocket size magnetic premium & gift ideas including Magnafolders, Magnaguides, Manaplay, etc.

Magnavox
I-40 & Straw Plains Pike
Knoxville, TN 37914
TVs, portable & console, black & white, mini, stereo, large screen color, portable radios, etc.

Majorca International
Special Marketing Consultants
137 East Hamilton Avenue, Suite 205
Campbell, CA 95008
Majorca pearl necklaces, earrings & bracelets, cubic zirconia, rings, earrings, sterling silver pendants, 14K gold filled zodiac pendants, etc.
For bank & incentive programs.

Manco Products
520 West 15th Street
Oshkosh, WI 54901
Motorized off-road recreational vehicles.

Manifestations Inc.
6361-E Yarrow Drive
Carlsbad, CA 92008
Unique shimmering metallic medium perfect for advertising, packaging promotions. Line includes business & greeting cards, annual report folders.

Marcel Watch Corporation
1115 Broadway
New York, NY 10010
Oleg Cassini quartz watches, Marcel watches & wall, mantel & desk clocks.

Marcy Fitness Products
2801 West Mission Road
Alhambra, CA 91803
Complete line of fitness products for the home. Weight machines, benches, bikes & barbells.

Oats Inc./
Graphic Shirts Systems
1119 Asbury Avenue
Ocean City, NJ 08226
Imprinted sportswear.

Sun Graphix
Mt. Hope Avenue
Lewiston, ME 04240
Featuring a collection of planning diaries, address books & leather accessories.

Sun Hill Industries Inc.
48 Union Street
Stamford, CT 06906
Desk & automotive accessories, clocks, health & beauty aids, etc.

Sunshine Industries
90 East Jefryn Boulevard
Deer Park, NY 11729
Imprinted plastic specialties.

Sunshine Products Inc.
40 Freeway Drive
Cranston, RI 02920
Knives, storage containers, bowls.

Suntana
Division of Sun Industries
1 Industrial Way West, Building B, Suite H
Eatontown, NJ 07724
Indoor & outdoor suntanning equipment & accessory items.

Suntex Incorporated
8060 I Northpoint Boulevard
Winston-Salem, NC 27106
Caps, emblems, embroidered corporate applique program, totes, aprons, etc.

Super Cooler Inc.
105 12th Avenue, N.W.
Waukon, IA 52172
Super cooler, beverage cooler with accessories.

Superior Gourmet Meat Co. Inc.
9701 South 78th Avenue
Hickory Hills, IL 60457
Steaks, seafood & gourmet food items.

Superior Toy & Mfg. Co. Inc.
3417 North Halsted
Chicago, IL 60657
Savings banks, gumball machines, gum & candy dispensers, card shufflers, tub toys, etc.

New American Library
1633 Broadway
New York, NY 10019
Paperback & hardcover books, weight watchers, cookbooks, reference, how-to, health, etc.

New York Steak
440 West 13th Street
New York, NY 10014
Serving cheesecakes, steak & smoked ham, imported jams & mustards.

Nikko America Ltd.
P.O. Box 235
El Toro, CA 92630
Radio controlled vehicles, boats, submarines & blimps.

Nikon Inc.
4433 West Touhy Avenue
Lincolnwood, IL 60646
Cameras, accessories, binoculars.

Nomadic Structures Inc.
111 South Columbus Street
Alexandria, VA 22314
The Instand 100 Series: folding, portable exhibit structures.

Nordic Ware
Highway 7 & Highway 100
Minneapolis, MN 55416
Distinctive ideas in microwave oven accessories, terra cotta products, electrics & heavy aluminum cook & bakeware.

Norelco-Consumer Products Division
High Ridge Park
Stamford, CT 06904
Men's & ladies' razors, personal care products, health care products, home products, etc.

Normark Corporation
1710 East 78th Street
Minneapolis, MN 55423
Fiskars, scissors & cutlery, knives, sporting goods, hand tools.

Norse Products Inc.
70-49 Austin Street
Forest Hills, NY 11375
Break resistant barware.

North American Premiums Inc.
30 West Waukena Avenue
Oceanside, NY 11572
Solid brass coasters, paperweights, buckles, license plate frames, keychains, etc.

Artistic Greetings Inc.
One Artistic Plaza
Elmira, NY 14901
Personalized premiums from $1.50 In-The-Mail.
Personalized stationery, name labels, etc. Custom Design programs, our products or yours.

Artistic Silver Ltd.
45 Montebello Road
Warwick, RI 02886
Awards, trophies, art reproductions, paintings, sculpture emblems, insignias.

ARTPLY Co. Inc.
518 Wortman Avenue
Brooklyn, NY 11208
Doll house kits, die cut alphabet letters & numbers, picture frames, markers.

Art's Toy Mfg. Co. Inc.
673 North 13th Street
Easton, PA 18042
Toys, stuffed animals, pillows, PJ bags, musicals, 5 ft. display animals.

Ashley Company
10 Harold Street
Sylva, NC 28779
Custom designed, manufactured & embroidered logo jackets of top quality satin nylon, corduroy & cotton blend. Also flags, etc.

Associated Mills Inc./Pollenex
111 North Canal Street
Chicago, IL 60606
Showerheads, foot baths, whirlpool baths, massagers, humidifiers, blood pressure kits.

Association of Retail Marketing Services
412 Ocean Avenue
Sea Bright, NJ 07760
ARMS, the national association devoted to the promotional needs of retailing.

Assurance Industries Co. Inc.
5353 Almaden Exp. E-47
San Jose, CA 95118
Watches, clocks, calculators, portable stereos & TV's, sunglasses, telephones, cameras, inflatable boats, etc.

Atari/Citidel
325 High Street
Metuchen, NJ 08840
Atari Home Computers & Atari software.

The Athletic Supporter Ltd.
27591 Schoolcraft Road
Livonia, MI 48150
T-shirts.

Atlantic Umbrella Co. Inc.
5036 Minola Drive
Lithunia, GA 30058
Umbrellas of all types, golf, beach, matching tablecloths & banners.

Atlantic Can Company
P.O. Box 119, 101 7th Street
Passaic, NJ 07055
Custom decorated metal toys, coasters, crystal cut styrene serving pieces, etc.

Atlantis Electronics
8625 Zetts Avenue
Gaithersburg, MD 20877
Electronic computer banks, AM/FM stereo receivers, electronic toys & wathces, etc.

Atlas Headwear Inc.
1575 West Walnut Parkway, P.O. Box 5646
Compton, CA 90220
Custom premium hats & caps with direct embroidery, lustre print, puff print, etc. Also visors & straw hats.

Aurora Impex Corp.
Aurora Plaza Hoiles Drive
Kenilworth, NJ 07033
Calculators.

Aus-Ben Studios
P.O. Drawer 1670, 411 Highway 105 Ext.
Boone, NC 28607
Quality collectibles & giftware hand painted in bronze and other mediums.

Austin Productions Inc.
815 Grundy Avenue
Holbrook, NY 11741
Sculpture, reproductions, company 3 dimensional replicas, ceramics & display units.

Authentic Models Holland
38 Hobson Street
Stamford, CT 06902
Historical executive hits, miniature musical instruments, shipmodels, ships in bottles, relics from past wars, etc.

Automatic Musical Instruments
104 Camelot Road, P.O. Box 1537
Clemson, SC 29631
Automatic player piano with 7 other instruments.

Avalon Ind. Inc.
95 Lorimer Street
Brooklyn, NY 11206
Crayons, chalks, watercolor, tempora & acrylic paints, hobby kits, toy kits, etc.

Avon Books
1790 Broadway
New York, NY 10019
Publishers of complete line of paperback books, reference, cook, sports, self-help, bestsellers. Customize to meet your needs.

Avon Sportswear U.S.A.
140 Cremazie West, No. 701
Montreal, Quebec, Canada H2P IC3
Apparel.

Azar International Inc.
31 West Prospect Street
Nanuet, NY 10954
Acrylic giftware & houseware, point-of-purchase displays, hot stamping & silk screening.

Azur Diffusions Corp.
PO. Box 9
Oldwick, NJ 08853
Memo pads, pens, key rings.

BTS Solid Brass Specialties
8001 Edgewater Drive
Oakland, CA 94621
Solid brass specialties, custom casting in solid brass, giftware line, solid bronze fine art sculpture.

Babyliss
7008 Fleury Way
Pitsburgh, PA 15208
Personal care appliances, curling irons, hair dryers, etc.

Bachmann Industries Inc.
1400 East Erie Avenue
Philadelphia, PA 19124
Electric trains & accessories, space age construction toys.

Balfour Company
25 Country Street
Attleboro, MA 02703
Customized jewelry, rings, awards, trophies, sales award incentives, plaques.

Ballanda Corporation
3926 Wilshire Boulevard, Suite 308
Los Angeles, CA 90010
Watches, clocks, calculators & electronics.

Bantam Books Inc.
666 Fifth Avenue
New York, NY 10103
Paperback books, cook, reference, sports, bestsellers, specially created books, hardcovers.

Bantam Industries Inc.
753 Larkfield Road
Commack, NY 11725
Smoker's accessories.

Barbara Creations Inc.
8121 North Central Park
Skokie, IL 60076
Sunglasses, imprinted sunglasses, magnifying glasses.

Crystal Electroni Enterprises Co. Ltd.
14/Floor, Mai Wo Industrial Building
90-98 Kwai Cheong Road
Kwai Chung, N.T., Hong Kong
Quartz & LCD watches, gift items.

Cuckoo Clock Mfg. Co.
Linden
32-40 West 25th Street
New York, NY 10010
Linden anniversary clocks, wall & decorator clocks, jewelry & music boxes.

D.G. Sportswear
5433 Eagle Industrial Court
Hazelwood, MO 63042
Fashion Apparel including jackets, T-shirts, youth items, aprons, tote bags, etc.

Da Vinci Group
Haunted House Road
Cornish, NH 03746
Fine leather goods, business, personal & desk accessories.

DAIWA Corporation
7421 Chapman Avenue
Garden Grove, CA 92641
Fishing rod and reel combos, remailer cartons, support materials, drop-ship programs.

CCC Book Group
Five Cedar Hill Road
Easton, CT 06612
Hard cover & paper back books, educational, dictionaries, cookbooks, trivia, leather desk sets & accessories.

CNK Importer Exporter
Super center Venancio
2000 SCA BL. B-50's/333
Brasilia, DF Brazil 70333
Hand gools, aluminum cookware, semi precious stones (rough), butterfly pictures & trays.

C&S International Corp.
600 Third Avenue
New York, NY 10016
Advertising calendars, porcelain collector plates & table mats.

CYRK Inc.
20 Blackburn Center
Glouster, MA 01990
Imprinted apparel.

Cable Electric Products Inc.
234 Daboll Street
Providence, RI 02907
Electrical & electronic specialty items, night-lights, cord reels, phone accessories, etc.

Calconix Inc.
28 West Lancaster Avenue
Ardmore, PA 19003
Pesonal electronics, watches, LCD & quartz, clocks, specialty items.

California Clock Co.
26131 Avenida Aeropuerto
San Juan Capistrano, CA 92675
Kit Cat Clocks & related items.

California Stuffed Toys
611 South Anderson Street
Los Angeles, CA 90023
Stuffed toys & dolls.

Cambridge Apparel Ltd.
1400 Aliceanna Street
Baltimore, MD 21231
Custom neckwear & accessories, hats, jackets & sweaters, embroidery & printed.

R. Dakin & Company
499 Point San Bruno Boulevard
South San Franciso, CA 94080
Stuffed toys, dolls, custom made plush animals, Christmas & holiday items.

Danville Import Co.
7 est 22nd Street
New York, NY 10010
Unique tools, specialty watches, promotional nylon bags.

Data Display Systems
350 East Tioga
Philadelphia, PA 19006
Novelty electronics, LED buttons, point-of-purchase displays.

Davar Products Inc.
15 West 26th Street
New York, NY 10010
Direct importers of promotional merchandise, clocks, trays, lacquerware.

Davidcraft Corp.
7040 North Lawndale
Lincolnwood, IL 60645
General merchandise, small electronics such as calculators, plush toys, housewares, etc.

A. David Design
366 Fifth Avenue, Suite 1012
New York, NY 10001
Hi tech attache cases, flashing buttons & other light up products, stationery items, etc.

De Beers Diamonds Limited
413 North Spring Street
Chattanooga, TN 37405
Jewelry.

Decor Noel Corp.
265 Belz Boulevard
Memphis, TN 38109
Christmas decorations.

De Long Sportswear
Box 189, 733 Broad Street
Grinnell, IA 50112
Jackets, caps, bags, embroidered or screened.

Dell Publishing
1 Dag Hammarskjold Place
New York, NY 10017
Harddover, paperback books, juvenile, reference, fiction, non-fiction.

Design Accessories Inc.
10 Shurs Lane
Philadelphia, PA 19127
Silk ties, gift certificates program, logo ties & scarves, aprons.

Devant Ltd.
P.O. Box 279
Monroe, NC 28110
Custom printed towels, tote & sports bags, shower wraps, bib, head & wristbands, stadium blankets.

Dial-A-Product
1666 New York Avenue
Huntington, NY 11746
A catalog library of over 760,000 promotional products from 59 countries.

Diamond Brand Canvas Products Inc.
Highway 25
Hendersonville, NC 28760
Soft luggage, sport luggage, day packs, duffles, totes, etc.

Butterfield Farms
330 Washington Street
Marina Del Rey, CA 90292
Fruitcake, cookies, popcorn, pistachios, jams & jellies, etc.

Buxton Inc.
265 Main Street
Agawam, MA 01001
Men'a & ladies' personal leather goods, belts, travel kits & calculator items.

Bynamics Incorporated
109 Railside Road
Don Mills Ontario, Canada M3A 3P5
Executive telephone communication products & adult hand-held games.

CBS Special Products
51 West 52nd Street
New York, NY 10019
Records, audio cassettes, video cassettes, certificate programs.

C.C.A. International Inc.
41 Madison Avenue, Suite 16A
New York, NY 10010
Dinnerware, chinaware, stoneware, mugs.

Camillus Cutlery Co.
P.O. Box 38, 52-54 West Genessee Street
Camillus, NY 13031-0038
Knives that may be hot stamped, imprinted, etched or engraved with corporate logo & used as gifts, incentives, etc.

Campbell Hausfeld
100 Production Drive
Harrison, OH 45030
Emergency Car Air Compressor.

Candle Corporation of America
141 West 62nd Street
Chicago, IL 60621
Candles & candle accessories.

Eden Toys Inc.
112 West 34 Street
New York, NY 10120
Quality plush toys, musicals & mobiles. custom design capability.

Edison Marketing Inc.
1270 Broadway
New York, NY 10001
Soundesign Consumer Electronics, tote bags, umbrellas, watches, tool kits, caps, misc. items.

Edmund Scientific Co.
101 East Glouster Pike
Barrington, NJ 08007
Scientific kits for children, telescopes, microscopes, astronomy books.

Egan Advertising & Graphic Design
1676 Ala Moana Boulevard, Suite 310
Honolulu, Hi 96815
Can of Hawaiian air and Hawaii sticker.

EHCO, Ltd.
901 East Nevada Street
Marshalltown, IA 50158
Barbeque items, snack cannisters, quartz clocks, statue of liberty products, etc.

EKCO Housewares Inc.
9234 West Belmont Avenue
Franklin Park, IL 60131
Cook & bakeware, cutlery, gadgets, etc.

El Patio Products
114 West 11th Street
Kansas City, MO 64105
Barbeque grills.

Dictograph USA
3573 Walden Avenue
Lancaster, NY 14086
100 memory cordless dialer, add-on-dialer—100 memory attaches to home or business phones.

Diener Industries Inc.
20257 Prairie Street
Chatsworth, CA 91311
Custom designed, sculpted erasers, continuity programs, miniature plastic collectable figurines.

DIPCO Products Co. Inc.
807 Main Street
Hackensack, NJ 07601
Dip-er-do stunt plane and other flying objects.

Direct Video Marketing
Rte. 2 Lewisberg Pike
Frankling, TN 37064
Snap-a-Zoo, Sleep Beeper, Go Safe, Ice Chest.

Division Sales Inc.
640 North LaSalle Street, Suite 350
Chicago, IL 60610
Housewares, giftware, tools, toys, sporting goods, closeouts, general promotional merchandise.

Donihe Graphics Inc.
P.O. Box 1788, Rt. 1 Brookside Road
Kingsport, TN 37660
Catalog printing specialist.

Dorcy International
c/o Carlisle/Mather
2 Madison Avenue
Larchmont, NY 10538
Portable lighting products & garden tools.

Double-Brella Co.
1808 Walnut, P.O. Box 3775
Manhattan Beach, CA 90266
Double umbrella with two uni-chrome steel shafts, opens automatically, elegant mechanical pens, etc.

Doubleday & Company
245 Park Avenue
New York, NY 10167
Hardcover, paperback books, juvenile, reference, fiction & non-fiction.

Case Mfg. Co. Inc.
179 Saw Mill River Road
Flushing, NY 10701
Decorative metal canisters, glass storage jars, stationery products, outdoor patio serving items, spice racks, woodenware.

W.R. Case & Sons Cutlery Company
20 Russell Boulevard
Bradford, PA 16701
Pocket, hunting & household knives, scissors & shears.

Casecraft Inc.
2621 West Grand
Chicago, IL 60612
All types cases, attache, sample, computer, tool, foam-filled, etc.

Casio Inc.
15 Gardner Road
Fairfield, NJ 07006
Calculators, watches, keyboard, typewriters, radios, mini TV's.

Cazenovia Abroad Ltd.
67 Albany Street
Cazenovia, NY 13035
Imported sterling silver & silver plate jewelry, holloware & gift items.

Celebre Diamonds
2345 Millpark Drive
Maryland Heights, MO 63043
Diamond necklaces & earrings, rings.

Century Publishing Co.
1020 Church Street
Evanston, IL 60201
Officially licensed NFL, MLB & NBA magnetic standings boards & custom magnets, sports booklets.

Chadwick-Miller Inc.
P.O. Box 515
Canton, MA 02021
Giftware, housewares, gourmet items, Christmas novelties, mail order items.

Diarough
420 Madison Avenue
New York, NY 10017
Genuine uncut & polished diamond jewelry, exclusive accessories, designs.

Canon USA Inc.
One Canon Plaza
Lake Success, NY 11042
Consumer calculators, electronic, solar powered, battery,
electronic typewriters, personal computers & printers.

Canon U.S.A., Camera Division
One Canon Place
Lake Success, NY 10042
Full line of 35mm SLR and lens shutter auto focus cameras,
lenses & accessories.

Canterbury International
91 Shelter Rock Road, P.O. Box 253
Danbury, CT 06810
Hand painted & engraved family crests & corporate emblems
in needlework, glassware, stationery & jewelry.

Canvas & Leather Bag Co. Inc.
350 Fifth Avenue, Suite 5520
New York, NY 10118
Insulated picnic & lunch bags, portfolios, knapsacks, totes,
schoolbags, custom designs & screening available.

Canvas Products of Georgia
P.O. Box 2226
Augusta, GA 30903
Canvas, nylon & corduroy sport bags, totes & travel bags,
aprons & gym shoes.

Pierre Cardin Electronique
1115 Broadway
New York, NY 10010
Unique Pierre Cardin collection of radios, clocks, hair
dryers & curlers, calculators, etc.

Cardinal Glove Co.
1 Lisbon Street
Clifton, NY 07013
Gloves, work, garden, fireplace, drivers.

Carnivale Bag Co. Inc.
544 Park Avenue
Brooklyn, NY 11205
Importer & manufacturer of all types of bags.

Carousel Industries, Inc.
6340 West Oakton Street
Morton Grove, IL 60053
Antiqued or gold plated gumball machines, snack
dispensers, lamps, telephones.

Electric Button Co.
1232 N.E. 26th Street
Ft. Lauderdale, FL 33305
Flashing & musical buttons & badges.

Electro-Optix Inc.
P.O. Box 26204
Ft. Lauderdale, FL 33320
Lighted magnifiers, lighted ballpoint pens, travel mirrors, etc.

Elgin Clock
Elgin National Industry Inc.
1800 West Fullerton Avenue
Chicago, IL 60614
Clocks, weather instruments, gift items.

Elmo Mfg. Corp.
70 New Hyde Park Road
New Hyde Park, NY 11040
Complete line of Elmo Astron portable video equipment.

Emerson Radio Corporation
2345 Millpark Drive
Maryland Heights, MO 63043
TV's, stereos, VCR's, tape recorders, telephones.

Emotions
5150 Rosecrans Avenue
Hawthorne, CA 90250
Decorative wall accessories, giftware, toys & games, woodenware.

Emperor Clock Company
Emperor Industrial Park
Fairhope, AL 36532
Grandfather & small clocks.

Emporium Leather Goods Mfg. Corp.
28 West 25th Street
New York, NY 10010
Leather goods, attaches, travel, groom items, small leather accessories, etc.

Energy Electronic System Inc.
9486-8 Deereco Road
Timonium, MD 21093
Computerized briefcase that dispenses beverages & talks to you.

Energy Sciences Inc.
16728 Oakmont Avenue
Gaithersburg, MD 20877
Solar musical key chain & music boxes, safari hat, kenetics & solar calculators.

Doubling Cube
37 West 20th Street
New York, NY 10011
Clay casino poker chips, dice, backgammon, game parts, imprinting.

Dover Industria, Comercio
E Importacao Ltda.
Rua Prefeito Olimpio de Melo, 1460
Rio de Janeiro, RJ Brazil 20930
Plastic bags, imprinted, & shopping bags.

Dragon Enterprise Corp.
8230 Garvey Avenue
Rosemead, CA 91770
Watches, time pieces, calculators, radios, telephones, novelties.

Dreamweaver Needleworks
P.O. Box 781
Newport, RI 02840
Embroidered sportswear, executive wear and accessories.

Dri Mark Products Inc.
15 Harbor Park Drive
Port Washington, NY 11050
Artist color sets, permanent & watercolor markers.

DuBarry Fifth Avenue (Fla) Inc.
2240 Southwest 70th Avenue
Ft. Lauderdale, FL 33317
Pearls, cultured & simulated, jade ivory, personalized jewelry.

Ducane Heating Corp.
800 Dutch Square Boulevard
Columbia, SC 29210
Gas barbeque grills & accessories.

G. Duchin & Associates Inc.
727 School Street
Pawtucket, RI 02860
Stamped metal premiums, metal Christmas ornaments & personalized premiums.

Champion Products Inc.
3141 Monroe Avenue
Rochester, NY 14618
Imprinted T-shirts, sweatshirts, polos, shorts, jackets, etc.

K&R Instruments Inc.
1933 Premier Row
Orlando, FL 32809
Automotive accessories, health & fitness products & security products.

Kaleidoscope Inc.
1348 South Flower Street
Los Angeles, CA 90015
Nylon accessories, bandanas, painter caps, disposable lighters, all printable.

Kalimar Inc.
622 Goddard Avenue
Chesterfield, MO 63017
Cameras, camera outfits, lenses, video kits.

Kalki Do Brasil Ind. E
Com. De Brinquedos Ltda.
Rua do Oratorio, 2254
Sao Paulo, SP Brazil 03116
Umbrellas, chairs, key holders, toilet seats, fishing equipment, hardware, etc.

Karinart Ltd.
5621 North Middleville Road
Hastings, MI 49058
Stained glassware, pewterware, copper pictures, japanese prints.

Kaydee Handprints Inc.
Skink Hill Road, P.O. Box 448
Hope Valley, RI 02832
Linen tea towels, calendars, terry velour hand towels, placemats, wine bags, murals, etc.

Character Licensing Inc.
630 Third Avenue
New York, NY 10017
Raggedy Ann & Raggedy Andy products & images for premium use.

Charmglow Products
P.O. Box 310
Bristol, WI 53104-0310
Gas barbeque grills, electric insect control devices, room heaters.

Chaseline, Division of Chase Bag Co.
2900 Vance Street Extension
Reidsville, NC 27320-1677
Screen printed T-shirts, tote & sports bags, aprons, oven mitts, stuffed pillows, etc.

EMB Corporation
Division of Sonwa International Corp.
136 East Broadway
New York, NY 10002
Signs—vision computer sign, L.E.D. computerized electronic message boards.

Eagle Affiliates
101-01 Avenue D
Brooklyn, NY 11236
Thermal mugs, steins, tumblers with specialty advertising inserts, children's eating & drinking utensils.

Eagle Golf Inc.
4641 Peoples Road
Pittsburgh, PA 15237
Custom made golf clubs, display of corporate name, logo, or promotional slogan.

Eastman Kodak Company
343 State Street
Rochester, NY 14650
Kodak Photo & video products.

Easy Art Inc.
2103 West 10th Street
Eugene, OR 97402
Kits—refrigerator magnet, jewelry pin, Christmas ornament, wall plaque.

Ebeling & Reuss Co.
1041 West Valley Road, P.O. Box 189
Devon, PA 19333
Hand-cut, full-lead crystal, porcelains, dolls, ceramic giftware.

Ebert Sportswear
P.O. Box 21747
Columbia, SC 29221
T-shirts, polo & baseball shirts, caps, visors, beach towels, tote bags, baseball & coaches jackets, manufactured & silk-screened in our own plant.

The Echo Design Group Inc.
10 East 40th Street
New York, NY 10016
Scarfs, ties, handkerchiefs, mufflers, shoelaces, suspenders, custom designed for promotional needs.

Ecologizer by Westclox
Division of General Time, A Talley Industries
520 Guthridge Court
Norcross, GA 30092
Water filtration, air filtration systems.

Classic Markets Corp.
6689-L Peachtree Industrial Boulevard
Norcross, GA 30092
Premium sales management services for American
Engravers, Conair, Penn Athletic Products, Ricoh, etc.

Clay In Mind
9710 Distribution Avenue
San Diego, CA 92121
Personalized coffee mugs.

Clearwater Products
Ludbridge Mill, East Hendred
Oxford, UK OX12 8LN
Finest quality smoked Scotch salmon, mailed direct from the
U.K.

Dunbrooke Sportswear Co.
P.O. Box 430
Lexington, MO 64067
Leisure & athletic type jackes for men, ladies & youths
suitable for corporate identity.

J.G. Durand International
Wade Boulevard
Milvile, NJ 08332
Glassware.

Dutchess Farms
Old Indian Road, RD No. 1, Box 95
Milvile, NJ 08332
Glassware.

E.P. Dutton
2 Park Avenue
New York, NY 10016
Trade books, children & adult, self-help, how-to, business,
cooking, education, etc.

Dynamic Classics Ltd.
307 Fifth Avenue
New York, NY 10016
Executive gifts, health & exercise products, automotive,
luggage.

E&M Sales Company
1879 Old Cuthbert Road, Unit No. 20
Cherry Hill, NJ 08034
Tote & roll bags, nylon wallets, embroidered headbands &
wristbands, beach chairs, towels, pen watches, phones, etc.

Chicago Cutlery
5420 North County Road 18
Minneapolis, MN 55428
Kitchen cutlery & accessories, pocket & sporting knives.

Chinon America Inc.
43 Fadem Road
Springfield, NJ 07081
Chinon brand 35mm cameras, lenses, accessories, movie cameras, projectors.

Chocolate Photos
200 West 57th Street
New York, NY 10019
Imported Swiss chocolates that can be embossed with any design or logo.

Chronomatic Inc.
1503 South County Trail
East Greenwich, RI 02818
Enameled emblematic jewelry, keychains, solid brass gifts, ceramic & desk accessories, etc.

Churchill Container Corp.
10100 Santa Fe Drive, No. 112
Overland Park, KS 66212
Plastic fluted stadium cups, both custom imprinted & plain.

Citadel Industries Inc.
325 High Street
Metuchen, NJ 08840
Stock & custom level & point catalogs, incentive travel programs, sales incentive progrmas, mail-ins, etc.

CITIPAK International Inc.
1470 Peel Street, Ste. 2M
Montreal, Canada H3A 1T1
Electronic databoxes.

Citizen Watch Co. of America Inc.
Special Markets Division
1200 Wall Street West
Lyndhurst, NJ 07071
Citizen quartz analog & LCD watches, wall, table & travel, LCD pocket television.

Clairol Incorporated
1745 Phoenix Boulevard, Suite 200
Atlanta, GA 30349
Personal Care appliances, heated rollers, make-up mirrors, hairdryers, foot care.

Cloverly Enterprises Inc.
11 East 26th Street
New York, NY 10010
Collectors plates, mugs, steins, figurines & porcelain premium collectibles.

COBID Corporation
4940 North Sheridan Road
Chicago, IL 60640
Wood desk items, miniature trucks, imprinted sun glasses, golf & safety items.

COBRA Communications Division
c/o Premium Marketing Network
7101 North Cicero Avenue
Chicago, IL 60646
Modular extension telephones, cordless telephones, answering systems, speakerphones, CB radios & radar detectors.

COBURN Corporation
1650 Corporate Road, West
Lakewood, NJ 08701
Comprehensive line of decorative self adhesive items.

Code-A-Phone Corporation
P.O. Box 5656
Portland, OR 97228
Telephone answering units, feature phones & Tel-a-Modem.

Coin Creations
1650 West 180th Street
Gardena, CA 0]248
Money clip, key chain, pendant jewelry for all gold & silver coins, medallions.

The Coleman Company Inc.
250 North St. Francis
Wichita, KS 67201
Lanterns, camp stoves, portable heaters, jugs, sleeping bags, canoes, fishing boats, air mattresses, etc.

Collector's Armoury Inc.
800 Slaters Lane, P.O. Box 1061
Alexandria, VA 22313
Full sized "non-firing" replicas of the world's most famous firearms, medieval & Samurai swords, suits of armour, military collectibles.

Collegiate Pacific
81 Adams Drive
Totowa, NJ 07512
Imprinted sporswear, T-shirts, fleece wear, jackets, shorts, pennants, hats & visors.

Colores International Inc
1405 132nd Avenue NE, No. 2
Bellevue, WA 98005
Windsocks, sport totes, keyrings & auto accessories.

Colton Industries Inc.
216 East Second Street
Mineola, NY 11501
Electronic & battery powered chord organs, cordless air gun, emergency car care kit.

Columbia Telecommunications Group Inc.
38 Roosevelt Avenue
Valley Stream, NY 11581
Novelty phones, animal phones & car phones.

Commodore Business Machines Inc.
1200 Wilson Drive
West Chester, PA 19380
A full line of microcomputers, peripherals & software.

Conair Corporation CM Corp.
6689-L Peachtree Industrial Boulevard
Norcross, GA 30092
Personal Care, health products, hair dryers, curling irons, hair setters, water purifiers, make-up mirrors, full line of telephones.

Concepts Unlimited Inc.
One Market Place
Mashpee, MA 02649
Emblematic ceramics & glassware, woven ribbon products.

Concord Camera
1463 Pinewood Street
Rahway, NJ 07065
Pocket, disc & 35mm cameras & accessories.

Conesco Merchandising Corp.
6260 Northwest Highway
Chicago, IL 60631
Watches, LCD items, TV's, fiber optic lamps, sunglasses, umbrellas, housewares, plush toys, etc.

CONMAK
161 Sturt Street
South Melbourne
Victoria, Australia
Apparel & accessories, candles, pottery, flags, furs, giftware, jewelry, leather goods, etc.

Connecticut Valley Arms
520 Wet 15th Street
Oshkosh, WI 54901
Replica firearms.

Consumer Guide® Publications
3841 West Oakton Street
Skokie, IL 60076
Variety of publications, including Consumer Guide books, new brand line of calendars & engagement books for 1986.

Container Corporation of America
400 East North Avenue
Carol Stream, IL 60188
Custom designed and manufactured, printed paperboard premium ideas for a variety of applications.

Container Technologies Inc.
12 Commercial Avenue
Barrington, IL 60010
Metallic & latex balloons, life size posters.

Contempra Industries Inc.
Division of Thomas Industries
371 Essex Road
Tinton Falls, NJ 07753
Indoor & outdoor electric electric grills.

Continental Camera & Communications Corp.
1100 Milik Street
Carteret, NJ 07008
Cameras.

Continental Carlisle
12 NE 36th Street
Oklahoma City, OK 73105
Tumblers, pitchers, coffee mugs, ice tubs, tip trays, tray caddies, etc.

Continental Extrusion Corporation
2 Endo Boulevard
Garden City, NY 11530
A complete line of hi and low-density carrier polyethylene bags for promotional use.

Converse Inc.
55 Fordham Road
Wilmington, MA 01887
Footwear products.

Cook'n Cajun
520 West 15th Street
Oshkosh, WI 54901
Bar-B-Que smokers.

Cooper & Clement Inc.
7854 Oswego Road
Liverpool, NY 13088
American sport character steins, handpainted character steins, glass & stoneware articles.

The Cooper Group
Specialty Sales Division
P.O. Box 238
Apex, NY 27502
Hand tools, brand names Boker, Crescent, Lufkin, Plumb, Wiss, Xcelite, & others.

Cooper Thermometer Division
Reeds Gap Road
Middlefield, CT 06455
Culinary thermometers, household, patio, advertising, rain, propane gas gauge

COPCO Marketing Corporation
298 Main Street
Woodbridge, NJ 07095
Smoke alarm with rescue lights, no installation.

Corning Glass Works
Houghton Park EB-1-6
Corning, NY 14831
Cookware, dinnerware, glassware, microwave cookware, gift programs, sunglasses, etc.

Stanley H. Cornwall Traditions
170 Forest Street
Westbrook, ME 04092
Bath accessories, executive games, ceramic lamps, decoys, novelties.

Corporate Insignia Neckwear
966 South White Street
New Orleans, LA 70125
Custom designed neckware.

Fox Marketing Inc.
4518 Taylorsville Road
Dayton, OH 45424
Radar detectors, scanners, CB radios & car alarm.

Frankford Umbrella Mfg. Co.
325 13th Street (Third Floor)
Philadelphia, PA 19107
Umbrellas—golf, custom-made, beach, sets.

Freeman Shoe Co.
1 Freeman Lane
Beloit, WI 53511
Men's dress and casula footwear.

Gerald Fried Display Co. Inc.
550 Filmore Avenue
Tonawanda, NY 14150
Boxes, pouches, bags, displays, sales presentation cases.

Frontier Watch Inc.
875 Avenue of the Americas
New York, NY 10001
Complete line of watches, customized, clocks & promotional gift items.

Furs & Jewels Unlimited
1370 South 74th Street
Milwaukee, WI 53214
Luxury furs & jewelry, 14K.

Fyrnetics Inc.
1021 Davis Road
Elgin, IL 60120
Smoke alarms, wireless security systems, electronic digital scales.

GTE Consumer Communications Products
1100 Cleveland Street, 15th Floor
Clearwater, FL 33515-6987
Residential telephones & accessories.

GWI Corporation
317 Harrington Avenue, P.O. Box 144
Closter, NJ 07624
Manufacturers of emblematic cloisonne/enamel jewelry, awards & gift items.

The Gallery of Financial History
72 Pioneer Drive
Nashua, NH 03062
Framed original cancelled/non-negotiable stock certificates.

Galloway Plastics Inc.
550 Frontage Road
Northfield, IL 60093
Custom plastic premiums—5¢ & up. Includes mugs, picture frames, binoculars, product design.

Garland Industries Inc.
1 South Main Street
Coventry, RI 02816
Writing instruments, desk sets, executive gifts.

Garrity Industries
14 New Road
Madison, CT 06443
Complete line of quality lighting & safety products, pen lite's, emergency flashlight pack, lanterns, etc.

Gazola S/A Industria Metalurgica
Avenue Julio de Castilhos, 1401
Caxias do Sul, RS Brazil 95100
Cutlery, bar accessories, hand tools, stainless steel flatware.

Gemco-Wear Inc.
One Gemco Plaza
Freeport, NY 11520
Food processors, coffemakers, coffee mills, stainless steel flatware, spice sets, replacement carafes, etc.

Gemstar International
3740 North Josey
Carrollton, TX 75007
Gift certificate promotion (gems & jewelry).

General Time Corporation
A Talley Industry
520 Guthridge Court
Norcross, GA 30092
Quartz & keywound travel alarms, wall & mantel clocks, barometers, air & water filtration.

Enesco Imports Corporation
One Enesco Plaza
Elk Grove Village, IL 60007
Dolls, clowns, musicals, brass, Christmas items, housewares, etc.

Enterprex International Corp.
3900 East Whiteside Street
Los Angeles, CA 90063
Time pieces, calculators, watches & clocks, lighting, etc.

Eppco Enterprises Inc.
12429 Cedar Road
Cleveland, OH 44106
Custom imprinted fender covers, seat throw protectors & hood covers, work mats, BBQ mitts, fireside accessories, etc.

The ERTL Company
Highways 136 & 20
Dyersville, IA 52040
Quality steel trucks, toy cars, tractors & model kits, microscopes & telescopes, etc.

EDGE International Inc.
P.O. Box 288
North Hollywood, CA 91603
Work & specialty lamps, stationery items for premium use.

ESKA Company
2400 Kerper Boulevard
Dubuque, IA 52001
Outboard motors, electric fishing motors.

Espirit Industries Inc.
18 Maple Street, West
Morrisville, NY 13408
Custom imprinted acrylic wall clocks & calendars.

Etching Industries Inc.
1001 Broad Ripple Avenue
Indianapolis, IN 46220
Etched crystal & glassware, logos. Coupon offers, custom engraving, etching machines & dies.

Ethnic Artwork Inc.
34090 James Pompo Drive
Fraser, MI 48026
Complete line of screenprinted & embroidered T-shirts, jerseys, golf shirts, etc.

Etone International Inc.
112 Bay Street
Jersey City, NJ 07302
Stuffed toys.

The Eureka Company
1201 East Bell Street
Bloomington, IL 61701
Eureka vacuum cleaners.

Evans Furs
2345 Millpark Drive
Maryland Heights, MO 63043
Fox coats & jackets, mink coats & jackets, lynx coats.

Eva-Tone Inc.
4801 Ulmerton Road
Clearwater, FL 33520
Communication specialists in print & sound. Custom audio messages on soundsheets & cassettes, custom printing & mailing.

Evergood Marketing Corp.
(EMC)
38 West 32nd Street, Suite 1103
New York, NY 10001
Classic oak pants press, oak file cabinets, the almost disposable electrical shaver.

Ever-Ready Appliance Mfg. Co.
5727 West Park Avenue
St. Louis, MO 63110
Utility & serving carts, director's chairs, housewares.

Evertime Electronics (USA) Corp.
16371 Beach Boulevard, No. 151
Huntington Beach, CA 92647
Robot clock, watches, calculators, telephones.

Exaclair Inc.
311 West 83rd Street, Suite B
New York, NY 10024
Memo pads, date & address books, desk accessories.

The Executive Line Inc.
30 Church Street
Chatham, NY 12037
Custom molded & stack key tags, emblems, badges, desk items, etc.

Executive Travelware Inc.
34 West 33rd Street
New York, NY 10001
Custom-made luggage & totes, Von Furstenberg luggage & totes, Italian imported leather goods.

Exocraft Special Market Consultants
137 East Hamilton Avenue, Suite 205
Campbell, CA 95008
Promotion priced packaged knife & block sets, woodenware.

Expressive Designs
3411 SW 49th Way
Davie, FL 33314
Limited edition collector plates, music boxes, pictures & vases.

FNR International Corp.
300 Canal Street
Lawrence, MA 01840
HO & N scale electric trains, die cast metal trucks, tool sets, jig saw puzzles & custom playing cads, etc.

F.O.B. America, Inc.
153 West 27th Street
New York, NY 10001
Seiko, Lucien Piccard & other brand watches.

F.W. Leisure Industries Inc.
2401 West 1st Street
Tempe, AZ 85281
Mini cars, picnic benches/table, patio furniture.

Fenton Art Glass Company
700 Elizabeth Street
Williamstown, WV 26187
Sandcarved crystal products, handpainted blown glass lamps.

J.G. Ferguson Publishing Co.
111 East Wacker Drive, Suite 500
Chicago, IL 60601
Reference books, dictionaries, legal & record guides, medical guides, home & auto repair books, etc.

Fiberlok Inc.
1520 Washington Avenue, 7th Floor
St. Louis, MO 63103
Iron on flock transfers.

Michael C. Fina Co.
580 Fifth Avenue
New York, NY 10036
Awards programs—service, safety, incentive. advertising specialties.

First Alert by Pittway
780 McClure Road
Aurora, IL 60504-2495
Smoke detectors, fire extinguishers, lighting/environmental controls.

First Pullman Corp.
1821 B Margaret Avenue
Annapolis, MD 21401
Leather attaches, folios & luggage, nylon & rubberized sport & accessory bags, semi-precious stones & jewelry.

L.L. Fischer Co. Inc.
212 Galt Street
New Albany, IN 47160
Award plaques.

Fisher Electronics/
Premco Associates Inc.
510 Zenith Drive
Glenview, IL 60025
Stereo & electronic equipment.

Fit-All Sportswear
Cook School Road
Pilot Mountain, NC 27041
Basic headband, wristbands, leg warmers, etc.

Chapter Sixteen

The S.R.D.S. Spot Telvision Directory.

If you're serious about starting a Mail-Order TV Company, then the following directory is a must. It lists all the TV stations in the U.S. and the General Sales Managers of each station. Write S.R.D.S. and ask them to sent you an application so you can purchase a copy of "Spot Television".

Standard Rate & Data Service, Inc.
3004 Glenview Road
Wilmette, Ill. 60091
(312) 256-6067

The official name of the directory is: Spot Television Rates and Data.

JOIN THE FUN!